ENDORSEMENTS

"***HeartBRAKES*** is a shame-illuminating tool that helps readers reflect, learn, and grow through relationship hardships. This well-organized book proves useful regardless of your current relationship status. This must-read book adds together biblical principles and relatable struggles to equal freedom from heartbreak shame."

TRACI COLLINS
MS, LCMHC, NCC

"The truth, transparency, and revelation revealed in this book will bring God's healing to the wounded soul. You will not be able to put it down! It is engaging and speaks to anyone who has ever experienced a heartbreak. Get ready to be transformed. The best is yet to come!"

LONYA WIGGINS
MS of Science and Education, Rehabilitation Counselor, Author

"***HeartBRAKES: How to Stop Shame from Stopping You*** is a beautifully written work of art that draws its readers into the normalcy of heartbreak, disappointment, and all the emotions that accompany the experience of loss. Kristin is vulnerable, transparent, and honest as she leads others toward healing while continuing her own journey of growth. This book is proof that the wait is worth it! YOU are worth it!"

KEISHA SHAW BARNES
MA, LCMHC
Licensed Clinical Mental Health Counselor, Balanced Life Strategist,
Author of *Where is Your Tank?*

"Every person I know has felt relationship heartache, and Kristin does an amazing job of helping us deal with our aches before (and *after*) they lead to debilitating shame. Kristin writes with a heartfelt style that makes the counsel and recommendations much more palatable, even when living them out may be painful. I highly recommend ***HeartBRAKES*** for anyone who's dealing with the difficulty of healing from past relationships—stopping shame before it stops you."

BARRY DARNELL
Lead Pastor, *Mosaic Community*

"Finally, a book that does more than just pat our hand and say, "There, there." In ***HeartBRAKES***, Kristin Franks describes in detail 12 different kinds of relationship pain and how God can (and will) heal each one, if we let Him. In this beautifully vulnerable look at her own relationship journey, Kristin gives the reader a rare look behind the curtain of the heartbreak shame we've all suffered from at one time or another—yet couldn't quite find words for. Well, now we can! And what God reveals, He heals…"

KIM ALDRICH
Discipleship Coach, Book Mentor, Speaker, Musician,
Author of *DiscipleSips: Leaving a Jesus Legacy One Latte at a Time*

"Kristin's insights are a beautiful biblical reframing of some of the most tragic and debilitating experiences in human relationships. Clearly her healing has been deeply informed by the voice of the Holy Spirit and his presence in her life. In ***HeartBRAKES***, Kristin provides an attainable template and practical application for anyone who needs healing from relationship shame."

MARY ROBERTS
MA, Licensed Clinical Mental Health Counselor

HeartBrakes

How to Stop SHAME from Stopping You

12 Relationship Heartaches God Can Heal

KRISTIN FRANKS

HeartBRAKES: How to Stop Shame from Stopping You

Publisher: Selah Press Publishing, LLC, selah-press.com
Editor: Kim Aldrich, kimaldrich.com
Cover Art: Christine Dupre, www.vidagraphicdesign.com

ISBNS: paperback—978-1-953211-21-7, eBook—978-1-953211-22-4
Printed in the United States of America

Editorial liberties: Names of God and references to Him are capitalized, and satan and the enemy are lowercased. Names of selected individuals have been changed.

This book is dedicated to my loving parents, John and Mary, without whom writing my story would not be possible.

This book is also dedicated to anyone who has ever been disappointed by love, clothed in shame, and hidden because of heartache. You are deeply cherished and valued. What a story you will tell, when God sets you free!

CONTENTS

FOREWORD
INTRODUCTION

HeartBRAKE #1 1
The Shame of Dead-End Dreams

HeartBRAKE #2 7
The Shame of Hope Deferred

HeartBRAKE #3 21
The Shame of Staying Too Long

HeartBRAKE #4 33
The Shame of Rejection

HeartBRAKE #5 53
The Shame of Regret

HeartBRAKE #6 65
The Shame of Stigma

HeartBRAKE #7 75
The Shame of Toxic Cycles

HeartBRAKE #8 87
The Shame of Unrequited Love

HeartBRAKE #9 105
The Shame of Holiday Heartbreak

HeartBRAKE #10 119
The Shame of Seduction

HeartBRAKE #11 137
The Shame of Addiction

HeartBRAKE #12 155
Freedom from Heartbreak Shame

ABOUT THE AUTHOR
ACKNOWLEDGMENTS
NOTES

FOREWORD

Since 2008, when Kristin graduated from Global Leadership Training Center (GLTC), the training arm of Master's Touch Ministries Global, Inc., an organization which I am privileged to lead, Kristin Franks and I have maintained an unbroken fellowship. She continues to be a resource for subsequent GLTC classes on critical issues including human and sex trafficking.

HeartBRAKES was written from a rich bed of experience, spiritual and natural. Kristin illuminates pitfalls, pitstops, and weigh stations along the journey each of us travels at one time or another. I invite you to join Kristin and others on a powerful journey of rediscovery, healing, and restoration. *HeartBRAKES* will help you take assessment of the blessed gifts of redemption and saving grace that abound toward us in times of heartbreak, shame, and confusion.

In this book, Kristin Franks brings a fresh word to those who are weary by offering lessons from her own life and from ten years of counseling. *HeartBRAKES* is filled with practical reassurances and counsel found in God's Word. Jesus is the well from which Kristin draws healing waters to share with us. She encourages those who have experienced failed relationships; forgotten dreams; addictions (physical, psychological, spiritual); abuse and violence; previous opportunities lost but redeemed; failures and comebacks. Kristin advocates for the fulfillment of victories and legacies, for our contemporaries as well as for those not yet born.

Kristin points us to proven strategies that put the brakes on the enemy's works. However, she does not leave us there. A Bible-believing and experienced counselor, she points us to the fuel source needed to revive and redirect us. Kristin uses spiritual principles from herself and others who've walked the walk, and she speaks to us with fresh insight. Through it all, she brings lasting fuel to help us believe and see through the eyes of a timeless God.

Boldly, she challenges us to open ourselves up to the possibilities ahead when we walk with the Almighty, the redemptive power of Our Lord and Savior, and allow the free course of the Holy Spirit. He invites you to "put the brakes on heartache," stop the shame, drain away old and destructive fluids, and prepare for new beginnings. Time to yield to His grace!

Dr. Patricia Bailey
CEO and Founder, Patricia Bailey Ministries,
Master's Touch Ministries Global, Incorporated
CEO and Founder, Global Leadership Training Center

INTRODUCTION

Just thirty minutes into my plane ride, the announcement came over the intercom, "Due to unforeseen weather conditions, your arrival time will be later than expected. We apologize for any delays." My heart sank. Based on the scheduling change, I was certain I'd miss my connecting flight, which would disrupt some very important plans. Suddenly I was catapulted down memory lane in my mind, pondering all the sudden stops, dubious detours, and daunting dead ends I'd experienced in my life, most often in romantic relationships. Not only had I been through lots of setbacks, I'd also been gripped by the shame of them, which tried to overtake me every step of the way.

As I reflected on my journey as a single woman, it was as if the plane ride itself was a metaphor for my dating life: "Due to unforeseen circumstances, your desires will be delayed *again*." Grabbing my journal out of my carry-on bag, I quickly began writing out the series of life experiences that led me to this point. As numerous relational detours came to mind, I jotted them down, along with bullet points about the lessons I'd learned from each one.

On that delayed flight, with ample time for reflection, I experienced what people refer to as an "aha moment." It was a divine whisper in the form of a question that went something like this: *What if your relationship heartbreaks and related feelings of shame don't have to be your destination? What if all the losses you've endured and patterns you've repeated are actually valuable life lessons, meant to nudge you closer to Me and the kind of person I'm calling you to be?* "Yes!" I said out loud as the woman next to me squirmed in her seat and pushed her ear buds in tighter.

Several Scriptures began swirling in my mind as I eagerly searched through the book of Romans. Listen to what The Message version of the Bible says,

> *The difficult times of pain throughout the world are simply birth (growing) pangs. But it's not only around us; it's within us. The Spirit of God is arousing us within. These sterile and barren bodies of ours are yearning for full deliverance. That is why waiting does not diminish us; any more than waiting diminishes a pregnant mother. We are enlarged in the waiting. We, of course, don't see what is enlarging us. But the longer we wait, the larger we become, and the more joyful our expectancy.* (Romans 8:22–25 MSG).

Those verses I'd read so many times before were instantly illuminated on the page. As I began reflecting on my own experiences, as well as those of my friends and clients, I realized we have *all* encountered various heartbreaks in our lives, intended to re-direct us toward God and His sovereign plan for us. Throughout our life journey, God has been battling for our hearts to be healthy and healed from shame, so they can keep beating for Him *despite* life's despairing detours and dubious delays.

HeartBRAKES is about saying farewell to the pain of repeated relationship setbacks, heartaches, and dead ends that stop you in your tracks—so you can live a life *free* from the burden of shame. It's about healing from the rejection that tries to ensnare us and keep us trapped in disappointment and regret.

What is heartbreak shame?

It is the feeling of brokenness and pain
associated with recurring disillusionment in romantic
relationships
and the related traumatic experiences from those losses.

I've experienced heartbreak shame personally and persistently in my life. I've seen it in the eyes of my counseling and coaching clients. I've heard it in their stories. I've walked with them through it. Everyone who has experienced attachment-related injuries wants to know, "How do I stop the cycle of heartbreak shame in my life? "How do I find hope again? Hope that I will be healed, hope that I will fulfill my purpose, and hope that God *still* has a good plan for me despite all the discouraging delays and messy mishaps?"

If you are looking for answers to these questions, I pray you will find some helpful insights in my story. Through all my relationship detours, delays, and dead ends I have learned some powerful life lessons and found healing from the searing shame a broken heart can bring. In addition, God has given me His grace to persevere in the belief that He truly is sovereign and has a good plan and purpose for me *despite* all I have been through—and maybe even because of it. My story is not over, and neither is yours. Through each setback, God has taught me invaluable lessons I want to share with you—lessons of healing, courage, and hope—with an overall strategy for living a life free from shame, in spite of the heartbreaks you've endured.

Flight delays are divine reminders that life often doesn't go as planned. It seems to have taken double, and even triple the time I thought it would take to reach my goals. It seems that every turn has been marked with a traffic jam, sudden stop, engine failure, or detour that has turned me around and sent me in a seemingly different direction. At times I've wanted to cry out in frustration, "This isn't the way my life was supposed to be!" Sometimes I *have* cried.

Yet through it all I've learned that, many times, getting off track *is* the right track. Sometimes, the path going the other way *is* the divine path toward your destiny. You get the gist, right? The delays are an important part of the route, even though it doesn't seem that way in the moment. Often it doesn't seem fair, or just, or even the slightest bit beneficial for us or anyone else. Nevertheless, one pearl of wisdom I have learned on my journey is, "God's ways are not our ways" (Isaiah 55:8). His ways are much higher than ours, which means a lot of times they don't make sense *while* we're experiencing them—especially when our heart is in pain.

Each chapter in this book describes a particular heartbreak (and accompanying feeling of shame) I have personally experienced, or walked with others through as they experienced it. Along with these examples, I've provided opportunities for you to evaluate your own heartbreak, to stop your unhealthy relationship cycles, and to start the process of healing the unnecessary shame they've caused. Part of the journey toward healing and wholeness requires looking inward and digging deep within your soul. I believe when you give your soul a chance to heal, there is a freedom you experience that matures you and strengthens your character. Maturity and character development help you stay the course when you feel weary from the journey.

This book will teach you how to navigate life's detours without completely losing hope. It will teach you how to learn from loss and use it to leave a powerful legacy. This book is a unique blend of counseling and coaching principles combined. The combination of both processes will help you experience true restoration and a renewed passion for life.

I have sat with many people, listened to their hearts, and walked with them through difficult relationship losses. While I've had the honor of helping some people this way, others may never step foot in a counseling office. Whether it's because of fear, past negative counseling experiences, or simply because they don't have the money to pay for it, they never receive the help they desire. Every chapter in this book is a guide for people who may never make it into an office setting, who are in need of healing and encouragement right where they are.

This book is also for you if you've had counseling, but you would like more healing from shame. As you read through these chapters and reflect upon the heartbreaks you've endured, I hope you have the deep sense, *this book is for me.* If that's the case, I welcome you to the healing process. I will walk alongside you and personally counsel and coach you, with the goal of helping you feel hopeful about life and love again.

I encourage you to courageously identify your own heartbreak shame as you read about mine. Then I invite you to complete the brief exercises at the end of each chapter. The *Life Lessons* and *Shame-Stopping Scriptures*, if applied, will help you heal from the

shame your heartbreaks have caused you and give you a chance to create new patterns instead of repeating old ones. These new actions in turn will empower you to live the life you were created to live.

As you read on, I pray you are strengthened.

Life Lesson

No matter what you're going through,
It ***IS*** *possible to navigate your way through*
every heart wrenching detour, delay, and dead end with confidence,
knowing that God has a unique plan for your life.

My prayer for you is that from your painful place of shame you will be completely changed. And out of that change will spring forth new life. The kind of life that births creative ideas within you. The kind of life that inspires you to fulfill your dreams, be a catalyst for change in the lives of others, and leave a lasting legacy. Let's begin.

HeartBRAKE #1
The Shame of Dead-End Dreams

I awoke one morning gripped by the notion that my deepest desires and dreams had completely passed me by on the highway of life. My heart felt like a faulty car battery that could no longer supply the necessary current to keep the vehicle in motion. When a car battery fizzles out, the car can't go anywhere. That's exactly how I felt that day, as though the battery fluid in my heart was all dried up, and I was stuck in a rut of pain and regret. "Where did I go wrong?" It was an ever-increasing, sinking feeling that would not relent. If repairing my heart was what needed to happen, the cost seemed high and my hope-tank was on *E*.

Have you ever felt like you've run out of steam? Like your dreams have died and you don't have the heart or the strength you need to heal from the shame that clings to your soul? Do you feel as though you aren't where you should be in life? Or where you are supposed to be? Or where you *want* to be? Are you tired of driving through life with a heart full of disappointment and heartache?

Sometimes it all catches up with you…

The missed opportunities, the broken dreams, the painful choices.

The recurring relationship roadblocks.

The wrong turns, the setbacks, the delays.

The romantic regrets.

The unfulfilled longings, the mistakes, the detours, the dead ends.

The years of heartbreak shame.

The culmination of heartbreaks can feel like a ten-car-pile-up on the interstate of life. A *pile-up is* defined by Webster's Dictionary as "A jammed, tangled up mass or pile (as of motor vehicles or people) resulting from a collision or accumulation."[1]

Has your life ever felt like a huge collision?

One minute you're cruising down the highway, and the next minute you're slamming on the brakes, staring at a mass of broken dreams, regrets, and wrong turns behind you—and a wall of shame before you.

How do I navigate through this?

That was my first question that morning. *How do I heal from all the detours, delays, and dead ends while maintaining faith that better things are ahead? More* questions began to tumble through my brain. *How do I re-route myself through this pile-up? How do I regain ground after the setbacks and the regrets that seem so great? How do I accept the past and find hope for the future?*

Amid the heap of heartbreaks I reflected on that morning, one was at the forefront of the traffic jam: *the pain of another year that ended with a dead-end dream.* The loss of a romantic relationship that seemed to have so much promise, yet ended with a screeching halt. The string of past relationship heartbreaks felt so palpable that day, with the most recent one ending up at the top of the tangled mass of metal and steel parts looming before me. *What a mess,* I sighed, wondering how long it would take to clear up the heartbreak-littered highway of my life.

Do you feel discouraged from all the disappointments in your life too?

Are you tired of weaving your way through toxic traffic delays and personal pileups?

Are you worn out from perpetually pumping the brakes while attempting to navigate through the shame of dead-ends?

I am intimately acquainted with this kind of pain. My soul has been weakened by relationship roadblocks, exhausted from false starts and the energy it takes to keep pumping fluid into the engine of my heart. Toxic turns and traffic jams have left me feeling beyond worn out.

After reflecting on past dead-end dreams that morning, all my questions began taking the form of mini-conversations with God. Slowly, the disjointed prayers took shape enough to put into words, and gradually the words became ideas, which resulted in the contents of this book. My hope is that as you read my story, you'll experience healing in *your* story. In addition to experiencing healing, I hope the words on these pages will bring you closer to the One who created you and knows your story detail by detail—God Himself. I hope each chapter breathes life back into your soul, comforting you in your pain and giving you confidence about your future.

Consider me your personal tow truck driver—someone to carry you through your heartbreaks and subsequent shame, to a place of healing, repair, and strength. You are no longer alone on the side of the road. You are among the sea of countless others who have experienced similar detours, delays, and dead ends in their lives. That's half the battle, isn't it? Knowing you aren't fighting by yourself? One of the main reasons people go to counseling is because they are tired of struggling alone. They feel hopeless, yet they haven't quite given up. They need reassurance that everything is going to turn out okay, despite how it looks. Something nudges them to keep going, despite their heartache.

I want this book to jumpstart your *heart.* I hope these pages provide the fuel for your engine and the courage you need to get back on the highway of life with renewed strength to steer through the detours, delays, and dead ends with confidence and faith.

One important lesson I've learned is that dead-end dreams don't have to keep you in a place of shame and regret. You can ask God to heal the shame you feel for not reaching your goals by a particular time, or for making a wrong turn, or for losing parts of yourself along the way and losing hope for what you thought your life would be like by now. I encourage you to trust that whatever heartbreaks or dead-end dreams you have experienced, it's not the end of your journey. God is faithful to weave every disappointing, pain-filled experience together for good—because even the very heartbreak you're going through now is included in the *all* things of Romans 8:28 (see the upcoming Shame-Stopping Scripture).

We can also take comfort in knowing that through our pain He is continually shaping us into His image and likeness, and rerouting us when we lose our way. The Prophet Jeremiah says, "Behold as the clay is in the potter's hand, so are ye in my hand." (Jeremiah 18:6 KJV). What an amazing gift we have, to be held by and healed in His hands.

Life Lesson

When your dreams hit a dead end, God can reroute you toward your destination. Dead ends can strengthen you for the journey ahead. If you let them, they will teach you inner resolve.

Shame-Stopping Scripture: "All things work together for good to those who love God, who are called according to His purpose" (Romans 8:28). Reflect on this verse and write your way to a healed heart. What do you need God to heal you from?

____

____

____

____

____

I hope you're starting to feel a sense of renewed strength for the journey. If you're not yet, it's okay. Keep on reading. There are more lessons ahead that will help you learn to fight through painful losses, mistakes, regrets, and heartbreak shame. In time, you won't feel so alone or defeated by life's heartbreaking blows. Let's continue onward.

HeartBRAKE #2
The Shame of Hope Deferred

I've had my share of romantic heartbreaks, and I can relate to the toll they take on one's heart. When I became a Christian in my early twenties, God gave me an invitation that set my heart on fire. It was an invitation to get to know Him in a way I had never known Him before. I opened the bible to the gospel of John and read the scripture, "My sheep know my voice and they follow Me" (John 10:27). I told God I wanted to be one of His sheep and He said, "I want you to be mine too, Kristin, and anyone who confesses me (The Lord Jesus) with their mouth and believes in their heart God raised Him from the dead, shall be saved." (Romans 10:9) When I accepted this invitation, I thought it included a formula for faith that would produce immediate outcomes to my prayers. In fact, I was convinced I'd be living the life of my dreams within a few short years.

What was the life I dreamt of? To own my own business, become a published author, meet the man of my dreams, get married, start a family, and travel the world. I was very excited about my newfound faith and read many scriptures about how God communicated with people in very direct and specific ways. So naturally, I started to believe that God was going to be specific when giving me details regarding my heart's desires and plans. After all, I now had a connection with God that I'd never had before. He'd issued an invitation and I had accepted. Surely He was going to bless me for this, right?

The first story of heartbreak shame I'm going to share with you is a peek into the heart of someone who believed that if you had just the "right" amount of faith, God would do anything for you, exactly when you asked Him to—including meeting the deepest desires of your heart—if you only believed He would. At this point in my journey, I believed God would literally do whatever you prayed for if you had enough faith. Like, for example, bring you a spouse right away simply because you wanted one.

My zealous faith caused me to take radical risks. I thought God was going to answer my prayers *exactly* the same way He did for certain people in the Bible. In fact, I thought He would be so specific that He would give me the name, date, and place where I would meet my husband. *Whoa*, you might be thinking, *God doesn't answer prayers that specifically*. You don't think so? Well, look at the story of Isaac and Rebekah in Genesis 24. Remember the servant's request? Abraham's servant asked God to show him who Isaac's wife would be based upon her response to his specific wish.

> Now let it be that the young woman to whom I say, "Please let down your pitcher that I may drink," and she says, "Drink, and I will also give your camels a drink"—let her be the one You have appointed for Your servant Isaac. And by

> this I will know that You have shown kindness to my master (Genesis 24:14 NKJV).

After reading about his faith and how he believed God could do anything, I thought, *This sounds like the perfect way to get a clear answer from God. I'm going to ask Him for the exact same thing.* Sure enough, when I was praying a few days later, I thought I heard God give me specific instructions about my mate, just like he did for Isaac.

Maybe this belief sounds silly to you, or at least a little far-fetched. If so, you would be surprised by the number of people I have talked with since I shared my story, who prayed and believed they heard God give them very detailed instructions regarding a relationship request too. Maybe you are one of those people—someone who was courageous enough to believe that God told you something loud and clear and you were willing to risk looking foolish until it happened. I'm talking about the kind of courage Noah had when God told him to build a huge ark to protect him and his family from the coming floodwaters, even though there was no rain in sight (see Genesis 6). I'll bet people thought Noah was crazy!

Because I didn't want to appear too fanatical, I decided not to tell people about my belief that God was going to show me exactly who my husband was. Instead, I wrote down his name on a piece of paper, folded it up, and sealed it in an envelope. That way, when my husband appeared, I could open it up and have proof of my answered prayer in writing.

I knew it was a big leap of faith to believe God told me my husband's name. I knew it might even be foolish faith, but I believed God could do anything. I knew He could do awesome things like that if He wanted to; I mean, He did it for Abraham's servant and for Noah and countless others, so why not do it for me? I continued to pray about the details of my husband's arrival, playing them over and over in my mind. Then, at the designated time I went to the place where I thought *he* would be—a little park near my home. I sat on a blanket under the tree and waited with bated breath. I knew his name, but how would I know it was him? I prayed silently in my heart for God to show me. Maybe *he* will recognize *me*, I hoped. Maybe God had told him *my* name too. Maybe he will walk up to me and say, "Hi, my name is_____; are you Kristin?" Just like Isaac and Rebekah. So,

I waited…

and waited…

and waited…

I waited and prayed, waited and prayed. The sun was slowly starting to set on the horizon. I began to feel doubtful. *What if he doesn't come?* I wondered. *Don't let your faith waiver, Kristin, or he won't come,* I told myself. I continued to wait. *How long do I wait, Lord?* I silently whispered that question to God…

But God didn't respond.

Not only did God not respond,

"He" never came…

That experience left me hurt, confused and ashamed. I didn't understand what happened. I *really* believed God had given me the name, date, and time that I would meet my husband. *Doesn't it take this kind of faith to hope for something you can't see yet?* I wondered. Sometimes you believe in something so strongly, like meeting your mate in a specific way, that it's heartbreaking when it doesn't happen. You have all the hope in the world you'll find someone out there you just haven't met yet, but when two years, five years, or ten years pass, your faith starts to waiver.

Or maybe your experience wasn't one of love deferred. Maybe yours was unrequited love, meaning you found someone you really loved, but they didn't love you back. Perhaps you believed in your heart that one day the other person's feelings would change, but instead, you watched them meet and marry someone else. I have experienced and heard examples like this from countless others. It's not uncommon to have faith that God will do something one way, only for things not to go that way at all.

Unfulfilled dreams or so-called promises from God turn our hope into heartbreak. Then comes the crushing shame and disappointment when these circumstances we've hoped for don't happen. You may struggle with sharing your pain with others because you're afraid and embarrassed about what people will think.

What do we do with these kinds of heartbreaking mishaps? The times we believe God is telling us to walk by faith on the water, so we take a big leap into the sea, only to feel like we're suddenly sinking. That's what Peter did when he said to Jesus, "If that's you on the water, Lord, bid me to come to you." When Jesus responded, "Come," Peter walked on the water by faith toward Jesus (Matthew 14:28). I thought I had "walking on water" kind of faith when I went to the park to meet my spouse—but soon I found myself sinking. Realizing I *wouldn't* meet my mate at a specific place and time was a challenging blow to my faith—one that required healing from the secret shame which took root in my heart. I also needed healing from the loss of who I thought God was.

I thought God was *specific*.

I thought God was *direct.*

I thought God would *answer my prayers when I prayed to Him.*

I even thought God wanted me to be *married by the age of twenty-five.*

But when that didn't happen, I had to re-examine my faith and ask, *So who is God really? And are His plans for me still good, even though they haven't worked out the way I thought they would?*

How many relationship heartbreaks have you experienced in your life? One? Five? Twenty-five? Whatever the number, you are not alone. The amount of people someone dates before marriage has increased because many singles are delaying marriage these days. It's not uncommon to expect multiple breakups, or more, in adulthood. It's much different than in former times when people married each other right out of high school and stayed together. My parents were high school sweethearts who beat the odds, got married, and are still married to this day. Their situation is rare in today's world. Nobody enters a relationship with the intention of it ending. So, when it does, it can really hurt. Heartbreaks take an emotional toll on your well-being. The shame and regret can linger for a long time—especially when you feel embarrassed about parts of your story. Then you begin to *hide more and more your story from others.* Shame caused me to hide for many years—I would only reveal parts of myself to other people as I concealed the aspects of my life that I thought I might be judged for.

The example at the beginning of this chapter was only one heartbreak in a series of many in my life. After taking time to allow my heart to heal from that experience, I embarked on another relationship journey. This time I met at man at church. Dave was in a leadership position and had a passion for helping others. I quickly gravitated toward his kind heart and enthusiasm for life. Every Sunday we would meet and discuss how we wanted to positively impact our community. We met frequently and coordinated several outreach projects together. I thought Dave was really spiritual. He always talked about his compassion for others and shared great ideas with me about how he wanted to change the world for the better.

Before long, I noticed Dave's interest in me was starting to grow. He asked for my phone number and began calling me on a regular basis. I was drawn to Dave's charismatic personality, his love for people, and his confidence in Christ. Before long, we started getting to know each other better through in-depth phone conversations. However, as we talked more, I noticed Dave began pushing for much more information from me. He was also laying on the compliments pretty heavily for someone who hadn't known me that long. He talked a lot about his readiness for marriage, what he wanted specifically in a wife, and how he could see us working together—*in his ministry.* I began to feel like he was trying to mold me into exactly what he wanted. I understood the importance of asking numerous questions to assess compatibility with someone you're interested in, but deep down, it felt like more than that. It felt like I was being *rushed and pushed.*

The other thing I noticed about Dave was that he didn't always respect me. For example, one time I told him I had plans with a friend, but he showed up at my house anyway saying he really needed to talk, asking me to be with *him* instead. This behavior of him expecting me to change my plans for him at the drop of a hat—was completely inappropriate. When I expressed my frustration, he got defensive. Then he apologized and gave me flowers the next day. I let it go, but I began to feel a growing uneasiness inside. We were just friends but he was acting like our relationship was something more. Overall, Dave seemed like a super-spiritual, super-nice guy, and he seemed to really like me. As time went on, I was feeling more uncomfortable with his actions, and yet, I kept second guessing myself. I'd just brush my feelings aside and think, *Don't make a big deal out of something that's not a big deal.* I really didn't want to get it wrong this time.

I decided to let go of the "name, date, and place guy" and opened up my heart instead to someone who was literally right in front of me. Seems more practical, right? No supernatural, God-ordained, park encounters this time. Just two people who consistently frequent the same place at the same time, with the same goals. It seemed to make total sense.

After I shook off the uneasiness and convinced myself I was overreacting, Dave asked me if we could go out on an official date. He told me he wanted to take me somewhere nice, and it would be a surprise. This event would be happening a little more than a week after he asked me to attend, and it would be a special time for us to connect and have fun in an environment other than church. Despite my previous feelings of uneasiness, I said yes. I was intrigued by what he had planned and wanted to be more open-minded than I'd been in the past.

The following Sunday before what was supposed to be our first date, I saw Dave at church with two little children. I thought, *That's interesting, I wonder whose cute kids those are.* When the opportunity arose, I walked up to Dave and asked him who they were. "Um, these are *my* children," Dave said sheepishly. "I was going to tell you I had kids…I just didn't have the chance yet." His response caught me off guard. Not that he had children, but that he hadn't mentioned them *at all.* I thought that was kind of strange, since we had been talking for a while at this point, attending classes together at church, and engaging in conversations at length.

That night on the phone, Dave and I had a more serious talk. We picked up where we left off at church earlier that day. Dave told me he was previously married and recently separated. I felt the hesitation resurface in my heart. What I initially brushed off as no big deal began to feel more important: his secrecy, his disrespect of my boundaries, his attempts to mold me into his idea of a mate, and the love bombing. Love bombing is a tactic someone uses in a relationship to win a person's affection and trust for their own gain, such as being overly complimentary or showering them with gifts, attention, etc.[2] As we continued to talk, the feelings of uneasiness returned once again. That night I prayed God would let me know if I was going down the wrong path with Dave.

The next morning—the morning on the day we were supposed to go out—Dave called to say he couldn't take me out that night because unfortunately "something has come up." I told him I understood and hung up the phone. After that conversation, I took a long walk. The more I walked, the clearer it became that *Dave cancelling the date was an answer to prayer.* It was just what I needed to put things in perspective. The ongoing uneasiness I felt was a gut feeling that something was off. Many times, we ignore gut feelings in the hope that things will work out. However, gut feelings are signals to steer us in the right direction. They can be heartbreak preventers if we heed them early on.

The next time I saw Dave at church, I told him I was not interested in pursuing a romantic relationship with him. I'll never forget how upset and angry he became when I told him. He was furious. I felt a cold chill run down my spine. *I think God may have just saved me from a bad relationship experience that could have really derailed me*, I thought to myself. Even so, I was disappointed that it was another relationship in which my hope was deferred.

Have you ever wanted something so badly that your heart ached from the longing for it? You know what I mean, right? I'm talking about that deep pain inside your soul that won't relent. The disappointment of an unfulfilled longing feels as strong and persistent as your heartbeat at times. Proverbs says, "Hope deferred makes the heart sick" (Proverbs 13:12). I understand that Scripture all too well. I have felt the deferment of many dreams in my life—the desire for a mate, children, healing from the past, and the desire for the life others around me had. I know the pain of having your heart's desires delayed. I also know the confusion of trying to sort out the difference between God's timing vs. self-sabotaging behaviors that can delay desires. This turmoil can be heartbreaking terrain to navigate through when you can't make sense of things.

At this point in my relationship journey, my heart had taken a few hard knocks, not to mention the heartbreaks I experienced *before* becoming a Christian (which I discuss in another chapter.) I thought for sure my desires were in reach. After all, "God is the giver of every good and perfect gift." That's what James 1:17 says. *So why was I still single?* I wondered. By this time, I was in my late twenties and ready for change.

Instead of trying to meet someone new, however, I took a step back, which allowed me to sense the timing for marriage wasn't quite right. As I pressed the pause button in my heart and stopped looking for another relationship (which had my pattern thus far), I decided to pump the brakes. That's when I heard God whisper, *Slow down, Kristin. My plan for you is different than you thought—different from other people's lives.*

It's such a gift when you can pause long enough to hear the voice of God and re-assess things after relational interruptions. Think about it. When your car starts making strange noises, you take it to the auto shop to get it checked out, right? So why should it be different with our life plans? When you are going in one direction and your heart starts making a noise (i.e., your plans are halted or you're feeling restless), why not stop and listen to the voice of God to get clarity and direction?

I used to think it was strange when people told me God would speak to them and give them direction in life. I didn't understand it, but I was also intrigued at the same time. I mean, if you knew you could hear from God and He would direct you, wouldn't you want to know what He would say? A good way to test this theory is to practice asking Him to speak to your heart and then listening for His voice when there is a detour in your life. God doesn't always speak directly to your heart, sometimes He speaks through a verse, or a song, but He *does* speak. Hearing Him speak brings the comfort of knowing He is with you, sovereignly guiding your life. What a gift it is to hear His voice.

As I look back now, I truly believe the roadblock with Dave was God's way of bringing more healing to my heart. He longs to heal our shame and rebuild our confidence. Sometimes while you are grieving a heartbreak, God will place your heart on pause—so it can be restored and steered in the right direction. Other times, He will take you through a longer process, not just a pause, but an entire season of transformation. This timeframe may involve deeper counseling and a transition out of your emotional comfort zone. Whatever the transformation entails, He knows exactly where and how you need to be healed.

I used to instantly gravitate toward the next dating opportunity when love stopped short. As soon as the relationship ended, I was on to the next one. However, an important lesson I've learned on my journey as a single woman is: *I want to be **healthy** more than I want to be **hitched**.* I want healthy heart alignment with my partner when I get married, and that's my desire for others too. You might be reading this and thinking, *That sounds nice, but how healthy do I have to be before I get married?* It's not wrong to desire marriage even while you're healing. You're not going to be perfectly healthy before you meet your match. No one is completely whole this side of Heaven. Yet it *is* possible to heal from heartbreak shame while you're single, so you can move more confidently toward a healthy marriage in God's timing for you. Wholeness is worth fighting for and available to anyone who wants it.

Life Lesson

When your love story comes to an abrupt stop, for whatever reason, it can often trigger shame. Yet your heart is resilient and will recover—if you let it. Take time to heal before you map out a new travel plan. Keep fighting for a healthy heart, the battle is worth it.

Shame-Stopping Scripture: Meditate on this verse and use it as motivation. "My heart is fixed, O God, my heart is fixed. I will sing praise" (Psalm 57:7 KJV). Journal any thoughts you have about how your hope has been deferred and how fixing your heart on God might help.

____

____

____

____

____

HeartBRAKE #3

The Shame of Staying Too Long

After the "name, date, and place guy" disappointment, the false start with Dave, and the pause to refocus on God, I thought for sure I was on the right track. After taking some time to heal and emotionally regroup, I was ready to take another risk in my quest for love. *Surely this time will be different*, I thought. I was determined to trust God's timing, yet hopeful I would find the right match soon.

One year later, I met Ben.

Ben and I were great friends from the start. It was a natural, easy, effortless bond. As our relationship grew, I began to see Ben as an inspiration, as well as a great friend who helped nurture and develop my faith. Our friendship continued to grow deeper throughout the first year. During that time, I started to sense his attraction to me was growing stronger. I liked Ben, but I didn't think of him as a potential mate. I thought he was an awesome guy, a man of integrity, and someone with similar values, but I didn't feel *eros* (passionate, romantic love) for him.

One day, Ben and I were sitting in his car talking when suddenly he blurted out that he had to tell me something. Of course, my curiosity was piqued. Before I had the chance to ask what it was, Ben confessed that his feelings for me had grown stronger, *and that he could picture me becoming his wife.* Ben told me he believed with all his heart that we were supposed to get married. Not only did he believe this, *he also felt like it was God's will.* Then Ben asked if he could date me.

My mind was spinning. While I loved my friendship with Ben and didn't want it to change, I was also intrigued by the possibility of dating someone I was good friends with. Based on what I'd read about relationships and heard from others who were happily married, I knew that friendship was a great foundation for marriage. *So why not give it a try?* I thought.

Even though I admired Ben's assertiveness, I still felt conflicted about his idea that our relationship was God's will, especially when I didn't have the same conviction. Here I was *again*, trying to discern which path to take. I started with prayer: *Lord, please show me if Ben is a good match for me*.

After I thought things through, I finally agreed to date him. I thought about Proverbs 18:22 which reads, "He who finds a wife finds a good thing." This scripture initially brought me comfort. Ben had indeed found and pursued me. Our friendship was rock solid. We shared similar values. It seemed as if God had brought us together at the right time. Yet despite Ben's certainty, I still had a conflicted feeling inside that I couldn't shake.

When we don't know which path to take, sometimes we ask for a sign, and that's what I did. After asking for divine direction, I began to believe the events that followed were indicators that Ben and I were supposed to be together. One sign came from someone I really admired who told me she was certain Ben was the one for me and I just needed to accept it. Another sign was an inspirational card from a friend, which included the very same verse in Proverbs 18 that came to mind when Ben asked if he could date me. Another sign was the matching gifts Ben and I randomly bought each other when we started dating. *What are the chances we would buy the exact same thing for each other?* I wondered. The "signs" seemed to affirm my decision to date Ben.

Looking back, I realize that most of the signs I received during my discernment process were *external cues*, rather than *internal promptings*. Internal promptings include things like a sense of inward calm, conviction, compatibility (i.e., how well-suited is this person for my life plans, goals, and personality), and the still, small voice of God that speaks to your heart. External cues include relying solely on how the person you're dating feels about you, getting advice exclusively from other people about your relationship, and outward physical signs. For example, seeing a rainbow that reminds you of a moment you shared with your partner, but can be interpreted various ways. A healthy balance of internal and external cues is helpful in decision-making. Yet in this case, I was relying more heavily on one form (external cues) than on the other form (internal cues).

Reflecting on this point in my journey, I now realize I had been groomed to put others before me. I only focused on the self-sacrificing parts of Scripture and applied them to my life. I would hear sermons on self-denial and think I was supposed to crucify *all* my desires in order to please God. I concluded, *God must want us to do the opposite of what we want, because our desires are selfish and self-centered.* Another statement I heard often in Christian circles was, "Don't follow your heart, because it is fickle and will lead you astray." I also heard, "Don't listen to your feelings. Feelings can't be trusted at all and aren't reliable when making decisions."

These statements led me to mistrust my feelings and disconnect from my heart on many occasions. I thought being a Christian meant continual sacrifice, suffering, and doing the opposite of what I wanted to do. Let me offer a little balance by saying there is some truth to this concept. Jesus does want us to love *Him* more than anything else. He says, "If any man comes to Me and does not have more love for Me than for his father and mother, wife and children, brothers and sisters, and even his own life, he cannot be My follower" (Luke 14:26 NLV).

However, God is not telling us to abandon absolutely everything we think and feel and become a robot. Jesus loves us and wants to provide for our deepest needs. Luke 11:11 says, "Would any of you fathers give your son a stone if he asked for bread? Or would you give him a snake if he asked for a fish?" In other words, God is saying, *Tell me what you want; I enjoy providing good things for you.*

Have you ever disconnected from yourself and your heart's desires because that's what you thought God or other people wanted you to do? I have counseled many people who don't trust themselves. People who don't know if what they think or feel is okay. They are always looking externally for direction and guidance. They are tossed to and fro with anxious thoughts because they think what *others* want from them is more important than what they want for themselves. I can relate to this because it's how I lived for many years. I constantly looked externally for answers and signs, apart from the simple guidance of the Holy Spirit within my heart. Always looking to others for answers will keep you stuck.

After Ben asked if he could date me, and I decided that all the external signs pointed to yes, that's when the self-convincing began. What is self-convincing? It's when you tell yourself over and over, in different ways, that you're doing the right thing. Even when your heart feels differently.

These are the things I thought to convince myself…

- *You and Ben have such a good friendship…maybe it IS God's will for you to be married?*
- *Ben is a great guy, and great guys are hard to find.*
- *Love develops over time. Besides, you don't need to have romantic feelings...*

In the beginning, I focused completely on the positives of our relationship and tried to ignore the other stuff, like the on-going restlessness I felt in my heart whether we were together or apart. At the time, I thought those emotions were "spiritual warfare." I convinced myself the negative reactions I had were attacks from the enemy, who was trying to keep me from following God's will. I was determined to follow Christ no matter what the cost, even to my own detriment.

I continued to push the negative thoughts and feelings out of my mind and focus on the positive aspects of our relationship. For instance, Ben was kind to me, we had the same spiritual beliefs, and we laughed a lot together. Ben also brought healing to my life, which was different from the heartbreaks I experienced *before* becoming a Christian, when I dated guys who used and hurt me. Back then, low self-esteem led me to stay in relationships with men who were selfish and narcissistic in nature. These men were not loving and compassionate like Ben, who was the opposite of those guys. Ben loved me with the unconditional love of

God. Ben's affection for me was wholesome and generous. I learned to value myself because of the way he treated me.

Over time, however, I started to depend on Ben more and more. I depended on him to lift me up and give me feelings of worthiness. I depended on him to boost my self-esteem and make me feel good about myself. Essentially, I began finding my identity as a woman in my relationship with Ben. I expected him to be there for me whenever I needed him to calm my fears, soothe my anxieties, and help me make decisions. His kindness and love consistently fed and fueled an empty place in my heart. One day I thought, *I need Ben to make it through life. He's always there for me, in ways no boyfriend has ever been there before.*

It's wonderful to be able to depend on someone completely. We need secure attachment with others to thrive in life. When you have someone in your corner who is trustworthy and reliable, you flourish. It's important to be in a relationship with someone who supports you, empowers you, and encourages you—that is healthy.

What is unhealthy is being in a relationship in which you find your worth and identity solely in the other person. When you start to feel as though you can't live without that other person and you need him or her at every twist and turn, it may be *enmeshment*, not love. Sometimes a relationship can start out as mutually supportive, yet become emotionally dependent over time. *Enmeshmen*t is when your decision-making and emotions are completely wrapped up in someone else. *Enmeshment* is also when your sense of autonomy is lost in a relationship. Two people are overly attached to each other instead of living life interdependently. It's not a freeing feeling. It's a trapped, isolating feeling.

As my relationship with Ben progressed, those deeper feelings that I wanted to feel about my life partner weren't developing. I just couldn't imagine him as my husband. I didn't feel excited when I thought about walking down the aisle with him and merging our lives together. I had a continual internal uneasiness when it came to marriage. At this point, however, I was very emotionally attached to, and dependent upon, Ben. The thought of ending our relationship terrified me. A few times I tried to tell him I wasn't sure about getting married, but anxiety stopped me. The fear was debilitating, yet I clung to Ben more and more, hoping my feelings would change and I would be able to marry him one day. We had been together for more than six years and had invested so much of our lives and hearts in each other. I simply couldn't imagine ending things and starting over again.

Over time, my anxious feelings and sadness grew worse. I excused myself from social situations and would break down in tears. I didn't want to tell anyone how I felt because I was afraid they would tell me to end the relationship, and I was scared to end it. I felt hopeless, lost, and stuck. When it seemed like I was wandering in the desert with no way out, I started to consider seeing a counselor for help. Simultaneously, I was in graduate school *to become a counselor.* Through divine providence, God led me to (and through) an extremely beneficial counseling process. Looking back, I realize God was preparing me for a deep inner healing that would take place in my heart.

The start of my counseling journey was a profound catalyst in my life and proved very worthwhile. I finally felt like I could breathe again. Starting counseling was difficult, painful, and arduous at times, yet so incredibly rewarding. Through counseling, I found the strength to face the truth that I didn't want to marry Ben, and then I began to work on letting him go. Two more years of healing followed, and my heart eventually shifted out of park and into drive again. I did get unstuck, but it required me taking a new path, including a move to another state and the courage to let go of yet another dream.

God was calling me deeper in my relationship with Him, which required an Abrahamic-like-sacrifice, and Ben was my Isaac. "Then God said, 'Take your son, your only son, whom you love—Isaac—and go to the region of Moriah. Sacrifice him there as a burnt offering on a mountain I will show you'" (Genesis 22:2, NIV). I didn't want to give Ben up because I cared about him so much, but I knew deep in my heart that I needed to let him go. It was a tremendous loss. Ben was a great friend and an important part of my life. We'd invested over seven years of friendship and dating before I finally faced the truth.

There are times when we invest large parts of our hearts, time, and energy into someone (or something) important to us, only for it to end. When a long-term relationship ends, it can be difficult to understand all the whys. It's easy to feel shame and hit the panic button, frantically trying to date again and make up for what seems like lost time. Or, you may want to block everyone and everything out, withdrawing into a cave of hurt and confusion. Whatever your personal shame-style, there is always a lesson to be learned. What I have learned from times of being stuck is that it was never wasted time. If you can shift your mindset from regretting the time you spent being stuck to trusting that you have grown from the experience, you truly can forsake shame and embrace peace.

After the heartbreak with Ben, I took another much-needed pause and refocused my energy on enjoying my singleness, rather than searching for a soul mate. At church one day, a guest speaker named Patricia Bailey spoke about her life calling to align with and empower others in developing countries. She talked passionately about her desire to train people to serve nations in various ways by meeting the needs of those nations. I felt something awaken inside my heart when she spoke. *Was I called to do this?* Maybe so. Since there was nothing holding me back from finding out, I decided this could be a fresh new start after my relationship with Ben ended.

After that divine relationship pause, I found myself listening for the voice of God inside my heart once again. It didn't take long before I felt prompted to go. A prompting is not necessarily an audible voice; it's more like a nudge you feel inside. It aligns with other things that are important to you. For me, it meant being with people from other cultures, and offering emotional and spiritual support to those who need it.

The more I read about Dr. Bailey's six-month program in North Carolina, it seemed like a great fit for my gifts and talents. Six months felt like a long time, but I was excited about the opportunity. At the same time, I was scared to leave everything I knew and move to another state. Nevertheless, I decided to go for it. *After all, what did I have to lose?* I was finished with school, renting an apartment, and working at a part-time job with no long-term benefits.

So, I did it! I packed my bags and moved my home, my heart, and all the hope I had left from Maryland to North Carolina, to immerse myself in a brand new experience. It was a new beginning. During that season of education and training, I spent time traveling to other countries, learning from the people there, and offering encouragement to those who needed it. God was molding and shaping my character by showing me how to share His unconditional love with others, despite what was going on in my life. He was revealing areas that I needed to grow and mature in, like how to continue trusting and following Him when all my hope had turned into heartbreak, and how to encourage others to do the same. This season was a precious time of growth and character development that I will never forget, a time when the Holy Spirit was depositing His nature deep in my heart to make me more like Christ—*His desire for all of us.*

Although this season was a wonderful part of my singleness journey, I still had a longing in my heart for a mate. Any persistent, unfulfilled desire can be painful to live with, whether it's a desire for marriage, children, healing, a change within yourself or a family member, or any number of yearnings within.

Although overseas ministry enriched my life in so many ways, I still found myself wrestling with this question over and over: *How do I continue navigating through life with all these unfulfilled longings and still have hope?* To this day, I am continually learning to trust this precious truth: **God has a sovereign plan for each of us that is deeply good—despite all our setbacks, regrets, delays, heartbreaks, and shame.**

After my adventure to North Carolina, I was in my mid-thirties, single, and starting to wonder if something was wrong with me. I didn't understand why I hadn't experienced what so many others had—meeting the right person, at the right time, with your values and goals aligned. Yet I knew deep inside there was a reason for the wait.

Have you ever wondered if something is wrong with you? Like something is broken inside that you can't quite identify, especially when it comes to enduring repeated relationship heartbreaks? Well, I want to assure you, **you are not hopelessly broken**. Sometimes we have recurring attachment patterns and unhealed heartbreak shame that require counseling to help us get to the root of things and become healthier. But that does not mean we are broken, it simply means we have more growing to do. Other times, it's part of God's plan for us to be single, even if it's past the age *we* had in mind for marriage.

Whether you're healing from unhealthy relationship patterns, or you just haven't met the right person at the right time, I want to encourage you—you are not alone. It may feel that way, but I can assure you, many people struggle with patterns they don't know how to change. Many people are gripped by shame and wonder If they will ever break free from it. Many people want to trust God with the desires of their heart but feel discouraged after so many let downs... I've been there *too.*

It's not easy, but as you muster up the courage to trust God once again with your deepest desires, He *will* steer your heart in the right direction—even when you've been in the same place too long. Clinging to the past in fear only results in prolonged stagnation, and staying stuck too long can be a source of ongoing shame.

Life Lesson

Prolonged patterns can always be changed with intentional effort and determination. God will give you the fortitude to fight when you ask Him to. Trusting God with whatever comes will result in forward movement toward your dreams, regardless of how you feel in the moment.

HeartBRAKE #3

Shame-Stopping Scripture: Reflect on this verse, " And he said, 'Take now thy son, thine only son Isaac, whom thou lovest, and get thee into the land of Moriah; and offer him there for a burnt offering upon one of the mountains which I will tell thee of.'"(Genesis 22:2, KJV). What might God want you to let go of in an act of surrender to Him, so you can move closer to the purpose He has for you?

___

___

___

___

___

HeartBRAKE #4
The Shame of Rejection

Have you ever seen an abandoned car on the side of the road?

As you drive by, you wonder... *What happened?*

Maybe it swerved off the highway unexpectedly. Or maybe the driver was in an accident. You search for answers as you scan for a closer look. There are many reasons why cars become abandoned. Similarly, our hearts can sometimes feel abandoned and rejected, just like a car can be left on the side of the road. One day you are cruising along in life, and the next day your heart is abandoned, uninhabited. You might be heading in one direction, and then suddenly veer off the side of the road not knowing what went wrong.

Sometimes you feel rejected by your significant other, like when a romantic relationship goes south and the person you're dating disappears. Feelings of abandonment can crop up quickly in romantic relationships when your partner ends the relationship and rapidly moves on to another person. One minute they are dating you; the next minute their social media pages are filled with pictures of someone else. We are in an era where blocking, ghosting, unfriending and deleting people are the norm. You can be talking with someone, thinking things are going well, and the next thing you know you've been misjudged, disregarded, or quickly replaced by someone else. Rejection has the power to stir up feelings of abandonment like nothing else can. Shame quickly replaces self-confidence as you get sucked into the comparison trap while trying to accept the fact that the one you love is now out of reach.

Perhaps the abandonment you feel doesn't stem from a romantic relationship; maybe you felt abandoned by your primary caregivers who neglected or abused you. Perhaps those who you thought would take care of you were unable or chose not to meet your needs. Many people feel hurt by their parents because they weren't cared for physically or emotionally in the ways they needed to be. If your parents got divorced when you were young, you may have gone through a difficult emotional process that has deeply affected your life. If there was addiction or trauma in your home, the effects are far reaching. Wounds from childhood are common because there are no perfect parents.

Feeling abandoned from any significant relationship can cause deep hurt and shame in your heart that can take years to heal. Sometimes one relationship heartbreak can remind you of previous feelings of rejection in your life. This secondary heartbreak compounds emotions, including shame or doubt about your lovability and self-worth. Each one of us has a deep desire to be loved and accepted fully, just the way we are. When we are living in shame, we strive to be loved by trying to prove our worth through achievement, which bids for attention. This strategy never works however, because we weren't created to strive for love. We were created to *be* loved exactly as we are. Yet the only one who can love this way perfectly is God.

What happens, however when you not only feel rejected by people but also feel forsaken by God? David felt neglected by God when he cried, "Has God deliberately abandoned me and forgotten his graciousness toward me?" (Psalm 77:9 AMP). Despite his hurt and confusion, he was determined not to turn his back on the Lord. A few verses earlier, David said, "I meditate within my heart, and my spirit makes diligent search" (Psalm 77:6 NKJV). David spent time searching his heart, and talking with God about it, so that he didn't suppress his pain.

The truth is, even though he felt rejected by God, rejection wasn't truly happening. God never abandons us. Even in our worst condition, we have the promise of His presence. "I will never leave you nor forsake you," Hebrews 13:5 says.

You never have to strive for His love. It's always available on demand. Don't let heartbreak shame keep you from God's love—let the pain propel you *toward* it.

Sometimes in life, we even reject ourselves. That's right. There are many ways in which *we reject and neglect our very own hearts.* I see this often in my work as a counselor and coach, and I have experienced it in my own life as well. When we don't take time to commune with our heart, like David did, we can abandon it. Sometimes, instead of facing the pain, you'd rather just avoid it, so you disconnect from your thoughts and feelings. You may not be aware of how much you intentionally separate yourself from your feelings. Maybe you are aware that you push feelings aside, but you don't know how to stop. Perhaps instead of dealing with your own feelings, you have a habit of rescuing other people from theirs, which in turn, keeps you from experiencing your own emotions. This diversion of your own feelings is a form of living in denial.

Looking back at my life, I can think of many times I lived in a state of denial and abandoned my heart to please other people. I didn't see the situation for what it really was or how hurtful it could be for me. Instead, I did things that weren't congruent with what was best for me. This inconsistency only left me feeling like an empty shell inside—rejecting my heart and what it truly needed.

Another way our hearts can feel rejected is through false or controlled intimacy. False intimacy is the appearance of a real bond where there's not one. Controlled intimacy is putting up strong barriers around communication and connection to the degree that interactions feel forced and unnatural. There's a facade in today's culture that we are all closely connected to one another. With the creation of social media sites—Facebook, Twitter, Instagram, Snapchat, and a variety of dating and chat apps—it *appears* that people are close and engaging with each other more. However, statistics paint another picture. They show that loneliness, depression, and anxiety are on the rise in the United States. Many people may look happy on the outside by posting attractive pictures on social media, but they are really hurting inside.[3]

Connecting with others through social media and texting has also left people feeling empty because they aren't engaging in real intimacy with others. The intimacy is filtered, controlled, and technological. Many people are searching for fulfillment, and even though their posts seem like they have found it, their hearts really feel *like an abandoned vehicle on the interstate of life.* Your status may say "in a relationship" and your timeline might be flooded with filtered selfies and funny memes, but your soul is telling a different tale—one that others aren't hearing.

It's easy to abandon our hearts through distraction, diverting ourselves from our true feelings and our moment-by-moment experiences. Let me ask you a few questions to see if you might be distracting yourself. Do you spend hours on social media, comparing your life with others? Do you paint a great picture of yourself and talk a good game to others, while silently suffering inside? Do you keep yourself busy so you don't have to feel emotional pain? If you answered yes to these questions, you are setting yourself up for self-abandonment. If you don't take time to connect with yourself, *your authentic self*, you will fall prey to living a life of heartbreak after heartbreak.

Your authentic self knows how you really feel. Your authentic self knows when to take a time-out and disengage from social media so you can *reengage* with real life. Your authentic self nurtures its dreams and allows them to grow. It also takes time to grieve personal losses and heartbreaks, instead of ignoring them or quickly moving on to someone or something else. Your authentic self won't stay in situations that are unhealthy for too long. Your abandoned self *will stay even to your own detriment.*

Here is a personal example of self-abandonment in my own life. When I became a Christian, I was zealous about my faith and wanted to find my God-given purpose as fast as I could. I read books such as *The Purpose Driven Life: What on Earth Am I Here For?* by Pastor Rick Warren and *Restless: Because You Were Made for More* by Jennie Allen. Both authors motivated me to discover what I was created for. I decided to become involved in my church, thinking that the more involved I got, the happier I'd be. The church was eager for me to participate, and several leaders approached me about heading up their groups. I was so flattered. I really wanted to help, and they needed my help, so it seemed like the perfect thing to do.

First, I joined the choir. Then, the homelessness prevention team. Next, I became a member of the global outreach ministry. Shortly after that, I became a co-leader of a singles group. Then, I joined another group, and so on. I felt included and important at first. This feeling didn't last long, however. Before I knew it, I was tired, irritable, and resentful toward everyone for pulling me in different directions. Why was I so mad at *them*? It wasn't their fault, it was my fault *for abandoning myself and choosing busyness over what was best for me.*

Instead of listening to my heart and using my gifts in a purposeful, intentional way, I ended up feeling overwhelmed and scattered as I dove headfirst into burnout. In addition, I became angry at God because I thought he was asking me to make sacrifices He wasn't actually asking me to make. After several months of dragging myself to church and feeling tired and worn out, I realized something needed to change. I made a list of all the activities I was involved in and how much time each one required. I spent time tuning into God's still, small, voice inside my heart. I asked myself, *What do I need to let go of so I can become more connected to my authentic self?* Then I paused and listened, so I could discover what to let go of and what to hold on to.

Life is always changing, and the things that are important to you during one season of life may change during another. Perhaps you want to write a book, for example. Writing a book takes much time and energy, which means some activities will need to become less of a priority. If writing a book is a priority for you, then that's what you need to focus on. Whereas in another season of life, your focus might be preparing for marriage, tending to a newborn, or starting a business. It's imperative to reconsider and reflect upon your life goals periodically, to get a sense of what you need to focus on, let go of, or make less of a priority. Consistent times of prayer and self-discovery are really beneficial when you are trying to evaluate your priorities.

Have you abandoned your heart recently? If so, did you abandon it in a relationship? In a career? At church? Maybe you started out with a desire to worship God but ended up worshipping a person or an institution instead. Maybe you drove yourself into the ground with too many activities striving for love and recognition, which is not a healthy way to live. Perhaps you abandoned your heart by tolerating things in a relationship that you said you'd never put up with. Or maybe you're in a vicious cycle of back and forth, up and down, ghosting and reengaging, blocking and deleting. Your heart is on "E." Empty. On the side of the road. You need a lift!

A dangerous place to be is in an abandoned car: on the side of the road, without fuel, vulnerable to being hit by another vehicle. An abandoned heart is just as dangerous. When you stop asking yourself what you want, what you need, and how you feel, you are vulnerable too…vulnerable to being taken advantage of by others. Vulnerable to living your life for someone else. Constant demands are everywhere in our society—demands for your time, your attention, and your gifts and talents. But what does your heart *need* to stay healthy? It's such a simple question, yet it's one we often lose sight of.

Staying connected to your heart and listening to what it's telling you through each twist and turn of life—even when it's hard has benefits.

We often want to escape the pain and avoid our feelings because it hurts too much, *but there is healing in feeling.* When we stay with the discomfort, and learn how to tolerate the distress instead of running from it, we can learn much about ourselves. Emotional distress passes over us like a wave in the ocean. It's just like throwing a bottle into the sea—what happens when you toss it into the waves? The wave will crash over it, but the bottle always resurfaces to the top. The emotional storm will eventually pass. When you weather the storm, your heart will teach you what it really needs. You will eventually learn how to navigate the rough waters to gain clarity. So take time to listen to your heart.

As you engage in this process of self-reflection, I am not promoting a lifestyle of self-centeredness or self-indulgence. At times, we want—and need—to make sacrifices for others. The key is learning to do so in a purposeful and balanced way . It's important to know how to care for yourself and your own heart *while* you care for others.

It's not wise to jump at every opportunity and respond to every need. It's not healthy to leap into a relationship and give it your all when you are receiving only breadcrumbs in return. God doesn't want you to burn out in your career, your ministry, or your relationship with others.

When have you abandoned yourself by giving your time away to movements, causes, ministries, and people, even though you felt drained and dissatisfied in the process?

I've done it repeatedly. I have abandoned my heart in relationships. In church. In my career. I have fallen prey to accepting jobs that were unfulfilling to me. I worked in jobs simply to pay the bills rather than live out my God-given passions. Right after I graduated from college with a bachelor's in psychology, for example, I scrambled to get the first job I could find, and that job was being a substitute teacher. I mistakenly thought that since I liked kids, teaching would be a good way for me to engage with them and make money at the same time. However, just because I liked kids didn't mean I was gifted to teach them. Teaching is a wonderful job when you're called to teach. Through trial and error, I learned teaching wasn't my calling. I found myself in a miserable situation; dreading going to work and living for the weekends but I kept thinking that I had to make a living this way. When you feel miserable at the thought of going to work in the mornings, that feeling is an indication that you may not be fulfilling your true purpose, that you're burned out from working too much, or that the environment is an unhealthy one.

Maybe you don't dread going to work, but when you get there, you're distracted or bored. You continually think of ways you *wish* you could make a living by daydreaming and making plans for the future instead of doing work that needs to be done. On the flip side, perhaps you're so busy during the day and so tired when you get home, that you don't even take time to dream anymore. Therefore, you feel disconnected from what you're passionate about and feel empty and lifeless inside. God didn't intend for you to work a nine-to-five job feeling passionless, purposeless, and depressed. He intended for you to use the gifts and callings He has placed inside you in a purposeful, passion-filled way.

God's calling is different for everyone. Have you thought about what it looks like for *you* right now? Ask yourself, "What are my talents and am I using them the way God intended me to?" When you are using your gifts and talents correctly there's a life force—a driving motivation—that's as steady as your heartbeat. It's a solid and stable rhythm. When you experience that sensation, you're in the flow of your calling. It may not always feel exciting or fun, but you experience an emotional stability and internal rest when you are on the right track.

Speaking of track, let's talk running. Long-distance runners fall into a steady rhythm during the second or third mile of their course. That's when they begin to develop their pace. That speed is what sets the stage for the rest of the run. Navigating the detours, delays, and dead ends of your life is similar. The pace you set, as well as discovering your gifts and using them as God directs, will continue to help you run your earthly race with endurance. That rhythm may get interrupted from time to time if you become disconnected from the dreams in your heart or if you start running on the treadmill of busyness or people pleasing. However, when you run the race you were created for, you will know it. Just like a long-distance runner, you will develop a rhythm that's right for you. You will find the pace that feels congruent with who God created you to be.

Knowing what God put you on this earth to do is essential. Additionally, it's just as important to know the *why* (the reason) behind the *what* (the action). Is your motivation God-inspired or people-driven? For instance, if you want to start a business, *why* do you want to do it? Is it because you are gifted to be an entrepreneur or is it to satisfy someone else's dream for you? What is your *why*? If you know your *why*, and it's not driven by others' desires for you, then you will stay motivated to do the *what*. The why supplies the fuel for the *what* to be accomplished. When I do life coaching with people who want to discover their purpose, but feel stuck, I help them identify the roadblocks that are holding them back so they can regain momentum and achieve their goals in life. To avoid abandoning the dreams within your heart, you must know the significance of three important words called your **VIP:**

Vision.

Intention.

Purpose.

The meanings of these words will help you identify your personal VIP in life. You are a Very Important Person, with a Vision, Intention, and Purpose. All you need to do is discover what these VIP attributes are and apply them. This knowledge is the foundation for continual progress toward your dreams. It also sets the pace for lifelong fulfillment.

Let's do some life coaching together to assess your VIP. Life Coaching is a process in which you answer key questions and then establish goals based on those answers. The questions in these exercises will be centered around your VIP. The most effective way to stay connected to your God-given purpose is by establishing a VIP for each area of your life.

Because this exercise is so important, I'm going to explain your VIP a bit more. The first part of your personal VIP is your *Vision,* which relates to your dreams for the future. Your vision, simply stated, is the mental picture of your life that you see when you close your eyes. Finding your vision—for any area of your life—requires you to tap into the creative part of your mind. Your vision is your God-inspired imagination at work. It's the part of you that was active as a child, but for many, becomes dormant in adulthood because of life's heartbreaks. Or it may be suppressed by your tendency to follow other people's desires for you, rather than your own. Take this book for example. I had a vision for it. I saw myself writing it and distributing it to others. That's how straightforward identifying your vision can be. Simply envision yourself doing something that brings joy to your heart.

The first question to ask yourself as you seek a vision for your life purpose is, "When I close my eyes, what do I see myself doing that stirs up passion inside me? Who do I envision myself being? What brings me a sense of enjoyment and satisfaction when I think about it?

Try starting with, "I see myself doing or being
____."

Write your thoughts here:

____

____

____

____

____

____

____

The next part of your VIP is your *Intention.* In other words, what are you going to do with what you see? It's one thing to see something—it's quite another to make that vision a reality. Many people have dreams and ideas they haven't acted upon. Listen to the people you know. You might hear them say, "I've always wanted to start a business, be a mom, write a book, paint a portrait, record an album, travel to a foreign land…but it just hasn't happened yet." If you find yourself saying or thinking something similar, and you need encouragement that you *can* fulfill your dreams, look to God and remember His spirit is full of creativity. He wants that for you too! He is constantly creating and desiring to create, *through His creation.* He loves giving people divinely inspired ideas. Why? So we can bring forth His beauty. Isn't that awesome?

Every song, blog, baby, business, and creative idea you have is a God-given gift. When you understand that God has given you *His* ideas, and when you know He wants to *empower you* to bring them forth, that's the fuel you need to keep on navigating through every setback and delay on the road to fulfilling your God-given dreams.

As you reflect on your vision, ask yourself what your *intention* is. Your intention is your action plan to bring your idea forth. Then, write one or two goals with timeframes attached to them, to help you carry out your vision. For instance, since my example was writing a book, here are a couple goals (intentions) to support that vision.

Goal 1: I will write one chapter each week

Goal 2: I will get my book to a publisher by November 2021

Write your own goals in the boxes below.

Goal #1	Timeframe:

Goal #2	Timeframe:

HeartBRAKE #4

Now that you have established your *Vision* and *Intention*, it's time to write down your *Purpose*. Your purpose is twofold. The first part has to do with your gifts and abilities. It's important to ask yourself, *Is what I want to do aligned with what God has gifted me to do?*

Sometimes people have the will to do something but not the talent for it. If you doubt this claim, just check out some early episodes of American Idol, and you will see that some of the people just weren't as talented as they needed to be. This perplexing tendency of having a desire without talent to match stems from a false perception of who people *think* they are, or who *others* think they should be. This mismatch comes from a place that is people-centered instead of God-centered.

Ask yourself, *Is what I see about myself, and what I want, truly in line with my God-given abilities and who God says I am?* For example, before I started writing I had to double check that my vision for the book was something God was inspiring me to do. When I reflected on what I am passionate about, I realized God has given me a gift of communication. Therefore, writing is part of my purpose.

Write your gifts and talents below:

____

____

____

____

____

____

____

To help you find your purpose, I also recommend taking a spiritual gifts inventory. A good one is found in the book *Discover Your God Given Gifts*, by Don and Katie Fortune.

The second part of identifying your *Purpose* involves identifying *who it is for*. This book was inspired by God's Spirit inside of me. However, I didn't simply write a book for myself. This book is for other people to be encouraged and strengthened by my story. Your gifts aren't for everyone but they are for *someone*. Who are they for? What kind of legacy do you want to leave? Think about the people who are a part of your vision.

Write your thoughts about who your gifts are for here:

____

____

____

____

____

____

____

The questions I've asked above as part of the VIP exercise can be applied to every area of your life. I recommend doing a VIP for your career, your relationships, and any other area of life that is important to you. Working with a life coach can help you flesh out your vision, intention, and purpose more if you need assistance. Additionally, when we take time to slow down and rest, it's easier to connect with our God-given dreams and goals.

HeartBRAKE #4

Our society is fast-paced and production oriented. I overheard someone say recently, "Americans are work addicted, and when we're not working, we are escaping through social media and various other obsessions." It's true. People in today's world are paradoxically results driven and easily distracted at the same time. We're expected to produce "hard evidence" outcomes in every area of our lives. Your boss, your personal trainer, your significant other, and your social media friends are tracking you to see what you're doing next. It can be emotionally exhausting at times trying to meet everyone else's expectations of you. Slowing down when you feel overburdened becomes crucial for your emotional health and well-being. Let's practice slowing down right now.

Take a deep breath.

Look at your surroundings.

The sights.

The smells.

Nature.

Breathe it all in.

Allow yourself to experience it.

Consider these words for a total of sixty seconds.

How do you feel? Was that easy or difficult for you to do? Psychologists call that exercise *mindfulness.* It involves meditation. For one moment, you can let go of the distractions, the technology, the people, the demands of life, the anxiety, and the to do list that rolls around in your mind. You can be present *in the present*, not thinking about the past or the future. Oh, how we need to practice this in today's world! We are always moving *so fast.* Always on the go. Yet God wants us to be present with Him, as He is present in each moment with us. This awareness, or being mindful, of His presence is an effective way that we can live purposefully.

In addition to being mindful, it's important to make time to have fun. One day I was talking to my counselor about how I'd been feeling depressed recently. As I was pouring out my problems, sifting through the challenges, and analyzing the obstacles, suddenly she said to me, "Kristin, what are you doing to have fun?" *Fun?* I thought. I didn't know. I had to think about it. She said to me, "Your homework this week is to go have fun." She was right, that's exactly what I needed—to have fun!

What are *you* doing to have fun? What hobby or activity makes you come alive? What brings you joy when you are not at work? Think of a way you can enjoy your life, and be present in the moment, by doing an activity you love. Write your thoughts about fun in the space below:

____

____

____

____

____

When you discover your VIP, it's like breathing life into dry bones. When any area of your life is barren and empty, it takes the breath of God's Spirit to make it come alive again. God told the prophet Ezekiel to speak over what was dry and dead, and breathe life back into it.

> Again He said to me, "Prophesy to these bones, and say to them, 'O dry bones, hear the word of the Lord! Thus says the Lord God to these bones: "Surely I will cause breath to

> enter into you, and you shall live. I will put sinews on you and bring flesh upon you, cover you with skin and put breath in you; and you shall live. Then you shall know that I *am* the Lord." ' " So I prophesied as I was commanded; and as I prophesied, there was a noise, and suddenly a rattling; and the bones came together, bone to bone. Indeed, as I looked, the sinews and the flesh came upon them, and the skin covered them over; but *there was* no breath in them. Also He said to me, "Prophesy to the breath, prophesy, son of man, and say to the breath, 'Thus says the Lord God: "Come from the four winds, O breath, and breathe on these slain, that they may live."' So I prophesied as He commanded me, and breath came into them, and they lived, and stood upon their feet, an exceedingly great army (Ezekiel 37:4–10).

What area(s) of your life does God want to breathe His life into?

____

____

____

____

____

Having a vision for your life is as imperative as breathing. With each new season comes new vision. With each loss of a dream comes the birthing of a new dream. It's an on-going, process. You are not too old or too young to create a vision for your life. You are not a failure. It's not too late in the game for you. There is nothing that can hinder you from fulfilling your VIP, except your own negative thoughts or behaviors that sabotage the process. The good news is, even those obstacles can be overcome if you are aware of what they are and how to defeat them.

I have struggled with many self-sabotaging thoughts when creating goals for my life. I have sabotaged my progress by lacking confidence in my abilities, by not trusting God to empower me through the process, and by procrastinating instead of pressing through the obstacles in my path. There are times I had a specific goal, such as writing this book. Yet I allowed myself to be pulled in fifty different directions, dismissing my goals to help others with their goals instead! There have been countless times when I knew I had to focus on writing and editing to make progress, but I got swept up in a friend's crisis or I chose to work overtime for my boss (a job that was helping someone else build *their* life-long dream).

What are your self-sabotaging behaviors? Take a minute to pray, listen, and write them below:

____

____

____

____

____

____

____

____

HeartBRAKE #4

No matter what your self-sabotaging behaviors are, you can overcome them. Each of us is on a unique journey, and God knows precisely how to get us where He wants us to go. Despite our missteps and mistakes, He knows exactly how to keep moving us forward. The key is staying connected—connected to His Spirit and to your own heart. If you apply this concept at every detour, delay, and dead end, you will ultimately achieve your God-given purpose.

Life Lesson

Don't abandon your dreams, and if you have, there's still time to get back on track and fight for them. Refuse to let the shame of unmet goals stop you from fulfilling the dreams that are in your heart.

Shame-Stopping Scripture: "Thus saith the Lord GOD unto these bones; Behold, I will cause breath to enter into you, and ye shall live" (Ezekiel 37:5, KJV). Meditate on this verse. What would it look like for God to breathe life into your heart again?

____

____

____

____

____

____

____

____

HeartBrake #5
The Shame of Regret

Have you ever headed to a destination without using your navigator? You might have a vague idea how to get there, but you're not completely sure. You mentally fumble around with the directions you looked at before you left the house, only to realize the location is not where you thought it was, and you end up on some back road…

Completely Lost.

Life can be like that sometimes, especially when you don't have a navigator. That's how I lived the first part of my life. GPS-less. No compass. No navigator. I attempted to figure things out on my own and got totally lost quite a few times.

In this chapter, I use the word n*avigator* to represent the Holy Spirit. The Holy Spirit is *God's Spirit* who dwells in us when we choose to turn our hearts toward God and away from living a sinful life. We receive the Holy Spirit when we ask Jesus to be in the driver's seat instead of ourselves. In the gospel of John, Jesus says, "I am the way, the truth and the life. No man comes to the Father but by me" (John 14:6). Jesus is the way *to* God. He is our divine navigational system. He provides us with the Holy Spirit to help navigate us through life.

Why do we need The Holy Spirit to help navigate us? Because God's word says, "Without Me you can do nothing" (John 15:5). We can't navigate through this life successfully without Him. He is also the only one who can lead and guide our hearts in this life, and into eternity, if we choose to turn away from sin and ask Him to be the Lord of our life. The Holy Spirit guides us in our decision-making process when we ask Him to. Jesus wants to direct us toward His purpose for our lives. He wants to steer us on the right path as we make choices about singleness, dating, and marriage. The Holy Spirit is a great navigator. He lets us plug in the coordinates, while helping to steer us toward *His* ultimate destination for our lives.

I've made many, many decisions without the help of the Holy Spirit. Those choices led to deep-seated feelings of shame and regret. My first memory of driving without a navigator is when I started dating Keith. I was a timid sixteen-year-old girl—insecure and looking for love. Do you remember your first crush? If you were anything like me, you were young and naïve, with no idea of what would be best to look for in a boyfriend. What stands out to me the most as I reflect on that relationship is Keith's personality. He was a rebel. The bad boy type. He was into skipping class and hanging out on the wrong side of town with the wrong kind of people.

Because I didn't have the Holy Spirit as my navigator, I was clueless about how to choose a healthy partner. I didn't know how to distinguish between trustworthy and toxic. Therefore I let Keith be the compass of my heart, instead of God. I thought since he liked me, I was supposed to like him back. That's how we started dating.

When someone expresses an interest in you, you need to know how to determine if you're interested in them too. If you are interested, you also need to know if it's for the right reasons. It's not the best idea to start a relationship with someone when you have no idea what you're looking for. It's like going to a restaurant and being served a meal without even looking at the menu and placing an order. Some people can be the wrong fit for you without you even knowing it. When Keith asked to date me, I hadn't thought about what I valued in a romantic relationship nor did I know how to choose a compatible partner.

It's important for women (and men too) to know how to *choose*, not just how to be *chosen*. You need to know what to look for and what to avoid. It helps to have a navigator, the Holy Spirit, to steer you in the right direction. Our earthly fathers can be great navigators when they reflect the attributes of our Heavenly Father. Earthly fathers can guide us on the right path by pointing out the good qualities versus bad qualities in a partner. It's important for fathers to play an active role in helping young women make the right choices in relationships so that they avoid unnecessary heartache.

I've worked with many women, however, who did not have a positive father image to guide them on their dating path. The person who was supposed to be a good role model is the *opposite* of what these women want in a mate. If a woman lacks that positive father role model, it's even more beneficial for her to connect with her Heavenly Father and let Him steer her toward the right person.

Sometimes, if you are like me, even with good guidance, you can still make poor decisions and have regrets. When I think about my relationship regrets, several come to mind. At the top of my list is giving my heart and body completely to a man apart from a marital commitment with him. When you give yourself to someone wholly (mind, body, and spirit) and the relationship ends, there's a deep severing of your soul, especially if the relationship was physical as well as emotional in nature. That scenario is what happened in my relationship with Keith.

One thing that attracted me to Keith at my young, tender age was his wild heart. He seemed carefree and spontaneous. I was the opposite—anxious and shy. He tapped into a side of me I hadn't experienced before. Unfortunately, I didn't see the other side of his character at first: the reckless, angry, unruly side. What originally drew me to Keith turned out to be a wrong turn that sent me reeling down a perilous path. Keith was super assertive when we met, which I initially perceived as a sign of confidence. However, I soon discovered he was actually insecure, unstable, and lacked a sense of purpose.

As a sixteen-year-old girl, I really didn't know who I was either. The two of us together were a recipe for disaster. Before long, I was making sexual decisions I was too young to make. I mistook sex for love and ended up brokenhearted and confused. I was not prepared for the emotional toll it took on me, especially when the relationship ended. I will never forget the day my best friend Terri called. Her voice was shaking as she inquired, "Are you and Keith still dating?" I could hear in her voice that something was wrong.

"Why do you ask?" I responded, as my heart sank.

"Because I just saw Anna wearing his football jersey," she stammered.

That was the beginning of the end. I called Keith and asked him about Anna. At first he lied, but finally the truth came out. He admitted he was cheating on me with her. I was crushed. It wasn't healthy for me to be in that kind of sexually/emotionally charged relationship, and I was filled with shame and regret. God healed my heart in time, but I could have avoided unnecessary hurt by relying on the guidance of a Divine Navigator. That shame and regret is what can happen when you don't have the Lord to guide you. Whether you are sixteen or sixty, when you don't look to your Heavenly Father for direction in relationships, your heart will veer off course.

Keith wasn't my only GPS-less relationship. I met Ted shortly after that during my carefree college years when I was skipping class and partying with friends. A group of us lived together and shared just about everything: food, clothes, cars, and lots of secrets. My erratic, fast-paced lifestyle made it easy for me to meet someone with a similar philosophy of life. Ted fit that mold, and he and I had a whirlwind connection from the start. Once again, I drove head-first into a relationship without a navigator. Since I did not have the Holy Spirit to steer my conscience in the right direction, I was quickly led astray into an unhealthy situation. Without a navigator, no one has the necessary coordinates to move in the right direction. If a person lacks those signals, it's easy to ignore things that would otherwise be clear indicators of a wrong turn.

For example, I knew the girl who had previously dated Ted, and I knew—prior to me dating Ted—that they had had a rocky relationship. In fact, not only were things rocky, I knew he had not treated this girl well at all. Yet, I chose to block that information out, thinking our situation would be different from theirs. Simultaneously, I was dating someone off and on who I didn't have the heart to completely end things with, so I decided Ted was my way out. Because of these other entanglements, we kept our relationship a secret.

Have you ever been in a secret relationship? There's a certain rush and excitement that comes from risky encounters. It can be thrilling but also toxic. This combination is what I felt like with Ted. We would meet late at night with a group of friends and then slip away by ourselves to do whatever we felt like doing. While it can be fun in the moment, there is an emotional cost to hiding things. Secrets and hiding create toxic patterns. There is an inner conflict that comes from covering up who you really are, and as you live a double life, you eventually lose the trust of the people closest to you.

After a while, people caught on to our secret romance, and we were confronted by others. At first, I insisted I only liked Ted as a friend. But eventually we stopped pretending and began sharing our relationship openly. My friends were understandably hurt when they found out I had hidden the relationship from them, and the inner conflict I had already, only continued.

In the beginning of our dating experience, the intense passion was exciting, but over time, I started to realize our relationship was based mostly on surface-level things like infatuation, physical attraction, and chemistry. In addition, Ted was starting to show some red-flag character traits. One of them was his tendency to lie, *repeatedly*. He would lie about where he was going, who he was with, and what he was doing on a regular basis. Deep down I didn't trust Ted because I never knew if he was telling me the truth or not.

One time I stopped by Ted's house to surprise him, and his roommate told me he was at work. *At work*, I thought? Ted told me he wasn't working because of his rigorous academic requirements and desire to graduate on time. I started reflecting on the times he and I had gone on dates together and he said he didn't have money to pay for it because he wasn't working. *Was Ted lying to me again*, I wondered? I was determined to find out the truth. The very same day, through no effort of my own, I found a parking receipt Ted accidentally left in my car. It was from the same location his roommate said he was working. I couldn't believe it. *Why would he lie to me about being employed?*

Possible explanations raced through my mind. Maybe he didn't want to pay for our dates. Maybe he was ashamed of his job. Whatever the reasons, I felt taken advantage of, so I decided to confront Ted about his pattern of dishonesty. Instead of admitting the truth, Ted continued to lie. He lied about his current job, about who he was spending time with, and other important aspects of his life. It was gaslighting at its finest. In case you aren't familiar with that term, gaslighting is a tactic that an abuser uses to make someone think they are crazy or just imagining things. Gaslighters want you to question your view of reality. It's a strategy that's used to *weaken* you so they can gain *control* of your thoughts and feelings. I knew in my heart something was off, and I was finally ready to accept the fact that Ted wasn't the truthful guy I'd hoped he would be. Instead, he was a very dishonest person who was leading a double life. I didn't want to be with someone who constantly lied to me, yet I kept hoping he would change…even though my gut feeling told me he wouldn't.

I tried to break it off, but Ted told me things would be different if I gave him another chance. I did give him another shot, but unfortunately, things only got worse. One evening Ted and I were at his house after a party, and before I knew it, we got into a verbal altercation. The next thing I remember was being pushed off the couch onto the floor. Immediately Ted said, "I'm sorry, I didn't mean to do that."

My memory was foggy the next day, and I didn't want to believe he had actually pushed me, but I knew in my heart that his behavior was abusive. I convinced myself that we'd both had too much to drink, and that he didn't mean to do it. I thought telling myself those things would help me feel better, but instead it kept me in denial, and the relationship continued.

The final straw was when Ted lied to me and told me he was going on a vacation with his family. I called him one night to tell him how much I missed him and heard several girls' voices in the background.

"Who's there?" I asked.

"Um, just some friends," he replied awkwardly.

My heart sank. It was the same story, different day. He was not with his family. It was another false story. Another lie. *How long will I put myself through this?* I thought. At this point, I realized it wasn't *him* causing the heartbreak, it was *me* allowing it. I might still be in that situation today if my Divine Navigator (the Holy Spirit) hadn't steered me on the right track.

Once I found the strength to end the relationship, I saw it for what it really was—abusive. Years later I became a therapist and learned more about abuse, and developed a desire to help other women identify signs of abuse in their own relationships. I know what it's like to experience this kind of heartbreaking situation. I understand the cycle of holding on, then letting go, then holding on again, then letting go again. Humans are creatures of habit and tend to repeat the same cycles. It's not easy to break free. Some people spend years and years of their lives enduring these kinds of ongoing heartbreaks.

Yet what I have witnessed, time and time again, is that God moves *toward* us in our pain, without judgment or condemnation, in passionate pursuit of our hearts. His sole mission is to love you and to draw you close to Him forever. He draws us to Himself by demonstrating what *His unconditional love* looks like and feels like. That's what He did for me. Toward the end of my relationship with Ted, I knew God's love was closing in on me. My heart was the destination where His presence longed to dwell.

Let me assure you, God loves you when you are hurting. He loves loving you through your greatest pain, patiently drawing you to the source of His love—Himself. Some of my greatest love affair moments with the Lord have happened in my deepest places of darkness and brokenness.

It was at this point in my life that God, my loving Father, began to navigate me back to His heart. He showed me what I *do deserve* and *don't deserve* from a man. I don't deserve to be lied to, cheated on, or emotionally or physically abused. I do deserve to be treated with respect, dignity, and honor. I deserve to be loved unconditionally by someone who loves God first, and who understands the value and beauty that resides within a woman. You deserve this kind of love and honor too!

Sometimes we want to be loved so much that we compromise our values. In a rush to get to the altar, we ignore the signs of an unhealthy relationship. I've learned that being healthy and whole is much more valuable than being married just for the sake of having a spouse and meeting the status quo. It's so much more fulfilling when you don't rush the process and wait for what's best.

After several heartbreaks without a navigator, I finally realized God had a better plan. He wanted to navigate me to His heart *first,* and from there He wanted to lead me in my romantic relationships. When I finally allowed the Holy Spirit, my navigator, to begin directing my relationships, things changed. I prayed to God about Ted and asked Him what to do. God made it clear that we were incompatible and going in completely different directions in life. Furthermore, Ted didn't have the character of someone I wanted to share my life with or marry.

When I had this realization about Ted's character, I had a choice to make. At first it was a difficult decision. I had been physically and emotionally intimate with Ted, which as I mentioned before, is a difficult bond to break. Despite the way he treated me, my heart and soul had been joined to his. When you are intimate with someone both physically and emotionally, it can cloud your judgment and make it difficult to end things when you need to. I tried to break up with Ted multiple times; but when I saw him, my heart would melt and I wasn't able to say goodbye.

However, as I consistently let the Holy Spirit love on my heart, I didn't have to do all the work myself. God started fighting on my behalf. He gently wooed me back to Him with His tender love until there was no more competition between Him and Ted. God's love for me won out. I could hear the Holy Spirit talking to me daily and gently nudging: *Let Ted go.* The more time I spent with Jesus, the more clearly I could hear His voice and gain the strength I needed to release Ted to Him.

One day I finally walked away. I was offered a new career opportunity in another city, which helped me break free from the temptation to stay connected to a man who didn't love God or me. I knew if I had stayed with Ted, I would have been miserable. Choosing a new path helped me heal from the shame of regret.

Life Lesson

It's possible to heal from the shame of regret. Wrong turns can't stop God's purpose for your life. When you allow God to navigate you, He will lead you down the right path. He truly will help you make the best decisions for your romantic future.

Shame-Stopping Scripture: Jesus says, "I am the way, the truth and the life. No man comes to the Father but by me" (John 14:6). Reflect on this verse. Is the Holy Spirit the navigator of your heart? If not, what would it look like for you to ask Him to be? If He is, how will you allow Him to continue taking the lead in your relationships?

____

____

____

____

____

HeartBRAKE #6

The Shame of Stigma

Sometimes our disappointments, hurts, broken dreams, and regrets weigh so heavily upon our hearts that we feel like we're running out of fuel—the fuel we need to stay the course. Have you ever felt this way?

You've lost hope that things will get better for you. Hope that your dreams will be fulfilled or your circumstances will turn around. It's heartbreaking to lose hope of ever reaching your destination. I empathize with the pain your heart has endured from driving on fumes. One unexpected detour in life that's especially tough is the battle with mental health challenges, like depression or anxiety, which abound in our world today. I have personally experienced both depression and anxiety, and the people I see in my counseling office every day tell similar stories of their own—stories filled with loss, disappointment, and pain from the emotional trauma they've endured.

Disorders such as:

- Chronic depression
- Generalized anxiety

- Bipolar disorder
- Obsessive compulsive disorder
- Post-traumatic stress disorder
- Postpartum depression
- Substance abuse
- Eating disorders
- Sexual addiction
- Other emotional or mental illnesses

Not only is the disorder itself difficult to deal with, but the stigma around it can also trigger feelings of shame.

Disappointing life experiences are sometimes the catalyst for the aforementioned challenges. Common events include the end of a romantic relationship, an untimely death, an unexpected job change or move, getting married, having kids, having a miscarriage, dealing with ongoing physical / health challenges, fighting a battle with addiction, experiencing trauma of various kinds, and relationship stress. Even a positive experience, like marriage, can trigger emotional hardship when things don't go the way you thought they would. Other positive transitions, like getting a degree, starting a business, or freeing yourself from a negative relationship can be exciting but also anxiety-provoking to navigate through at times. Circumstances aren't always the catalyst of anxiety or depression. Sometimes there's a chemical imbalance in the brain that leads to the clinical symptoms of a disorder. Other times, a chemical imbalance combined with circumstances may be the cause.

A particularly dark time in my life was when my mental health became compromised in graduate school. My coursework was heavy from the start, and at the same time, I had much inner turmoil about a guy I'd been dating for years. We were at odds about moving forward toward a deeper commitment, yet we didn't want to stop trying to make things work. The combined stress of going back to school and worrying about my relationship mounted.

Each day began with anxious thoughts and panic attacks, which steadily grew worse. I would sit in class and try to ignore the pain. The feelings became so intense at one point that I couldn't focus on what I needed to accomplish during the day. Life felt like an uphill climb. Instead of having the career, relationship, and dreams I'd hoped for at this point, I was enduring academic stress, relationship frustration, financial pressure, and confusion about my calling. Before long I was beginning to show signs of depression.

Days turned into weeks, which turned into months of distress. Lack of direction and the disappointment from unfulfilled goals ruled my mind. I started to feel purposeless. Passionless. Even hopeless at times. My faith was slowly waning, and I lacked the kind of intimacy with God that I'd had before. I was running low on fuel.

I could no longer deny my feelings or pretend they weren't as bad as they were. Finally, I called my friend Lori for help. She calmly talked me through the fear and said, "You will get through this. You just have to keep taking one step at a time, and don't give up." It was just what I needed to hear to overcome the fearful thoughts, instead of yielding to the anxiety.

Then she suggested taking medication for depression, but I was against the idea. The thought of taking meds made me feel like I wasn't a strong enough person. I wanted to power through it. I was determined not to let my emotions get the best of me. Yet as I pressed through the persistent pain, day after day, it still felt like I was driving on fumes.

If you've ever had this kind of experience, you know exactly what I'm talking about. It's a scary place to be. If you haven't gone through it before, it may be difficult to understand what it's like. Many people think depression is something you can just snap out of if you try hard enough, or just pray your way through. But when it becomes chronic and clinical, it doesn't work that way. During this season of setbacks, I was trying hard to navigate myself in the right direction, yet my fuel tank only got emptier and emptier.

Psalm 40 is the place in the Bible I would go to for comfort during this time. In this Psalm, David writes about how he waited upon the Lord, and about how God brought him out of a difficult season. "He also brought me up out of a horrible pit, out of the miry clay, and set my feet upon a rock, and established my steps. He has put a new song in my mouth—praise to our God; many will see it and fear, and will trust in the Lord" (Psalm 40: 2–3).

I wanted to believe this was true, but it was hard to imagine getting out of that pit and praising God in spite of it. When you are in a hopeless place, a place of despair and delayed dreams, it can be difficult to believe things will change. The Bible refers to coming out of a place of hopelessness as *deliverance.* According to Strong's Concordance, deliverance means freedom and liberty.[6] When God lifts you from a place of defeat into a place of victory you will experience a newfound freedom you've never had before. There are examples like David's throughout the Bible, and I encourage you to search for scriptures about strength when you feel low on fuel.

Why does God allow us to experience heartache and pain in the first place, you might wonder? I don't know all the reasons. I don't think anyone knows exactly why their life consists of the specific heartbreaks it does.

However, one thing I have learned is that God will use those experiences to make you more like Him and help you fulfill the purpose He has for you. Romans 8:29 says, "For whom He foreknew, He also predestined to be conformed to the image of His Son." Before you were born, God had a plan to mold you into His image. In the Bible, you see countless people whose paths of suffering helped to develop Christ-like character in them. God allows His children to travel unique paths of testing and trials, culminating in growth spurts that reflect His image and glory. Knowing this truth, and reading about the lives of those who had lived through it, brought me comfort during that challenging time.

For reasons I don't fully understand, the waves of emotion eventually went into hibernation and lay dormant enough for me to graduate and move overseas to live and work in Central America. It was during my travels that I discovered a vast number of people who struggled with depression and anxiety but didn't talk about it.

Many people don't want others to know what's really going on inside them because talking about it makes them feel weak and vulnerable. Much shame is still attached to mental health disorders, but it doesn't have to be this way. It's possible to be resilient even in the deepest pit of emotional despair. You are a fighter. If you're reading this book and have life in your lungs, your purpose on earth is not finished yet.

I returned from Costa Rica with a fresh sense of zeal and purpose. Just as I was fueling up for the next phase of my destiny, however, the sad and anxious feelings returned with a vengeance. This time, it was even worse than before. I kept thinking, *If I have just a little more faith…if I can hold on a little bit longer...I know I can get through this*, but the emotional pain was not letting up. That's when I remembered Lori's advice about considering medication.

I decided to make an appointment with a psychiatrist, even though I was skeptical. The waiting list was several weeks, and I was tempted to back out, but I asked the receptionist to go ahead and schedule me anyway because I was determined to get better. Those weeks of waiting were like driving through life with a beyond-empty gas tank, but *finally* I got a call to come to the psychiatrist's office.

The doctor was so kind and encouraging. After the intake session, she said, "Kristin, your anxiety and depression are at a clinical level. It's not something you can just snap out of. Medication could really help balance out your brain chemistry." The psychiatrist then assured me she would put me on the lowest dosage of medication possible, and that it wouldn't be something I'd become addicted to. She gave me two options to choose from, encouraging me to give one of them a try.

After our appointment, I felt more confident about taking something for my symptoms. Unfortunately, some of the advice I received from well-meaning church goers indicated that taking medication meant I lacked faith, and that *prayer alone* was the key to overcoming depression and anxiety. Although their opinions initially perpetuated feelings of shame, I knew taking medication was the right thing to do. The next day, I got the prescription filled and started my road to recovery. I did experience a few side-effects at first. Sleeping at night was difficult and my appetite changed a bit, but overall I felt *much* better. I was so grateful I'd chosen the path of trying medicine.

I want to add a clarification here: Sometimes medicine is the best route to take, and sometimes it's not. Deciding whether or not to start taking an anti-depressant is a personal journey that is unique to each person. While it worked great for me this time, at another time in my life I tried a different medication, and it wasn't a good fit for me. My body did not react well to it, so I decided to stop taking it. Every situation is different, every medication is different, and it's not always a smooth, easy path figuring out the best option. *Only you can choose the best decision for you.*

As I was adjusting to the medication and starting to feel like myself again, I began a new job search in the hopes of jumpstarting my purpose. Before long I stumbled upon the website of a counseling agency in the Charlotte area. I'd met the owners of the business at a conference several years prior and wondered if I might be a good match for their organization. Since then, I'd gotten a master's degree in counseling, but I hadn't seen or spoken to someone in the organization in years. I was convinced that the agency wouldn't remember me and felt timid about contacting them, yet something inside was prompting me to do it: *I have nothing to lose, I might as well try,* I thought.

That night I emailed the agency owners and was surprised to receive such a quick response. The director replied that one of their employees was leaving, so they were interested in hiring a new counselor. I told them I was definitely interested. To my amazement, I got a call back by the end of the week asking if I wanted to come in for an interview. "This feels like divine timing," the director said. "We were just getting ready to start looking for a counselor when you contacted us." I was amazed. Everything was happening so *fast.* I knew it was time for a fresh start.

The next day I contacted the director and told her I would come in for an interview. A friend offered to help me with the airfare, and I gladly accepted. In a matter of days, I booked a flight to North Carolina. I rented a car, mapped out directions to the counseling center the day before the interview, and barely slept that night. I was nervous and excited at the same time.

During the interview, I was in a room with ten other people, all of whom asked me questions at the same time. That approach is enough to make anyone nervous, whether you struggle with anxiety or not! The interviewers told me they would talk it over and get back to me soon. The very next day the director called to offer me the job. "The only thing is, we'd need you to start right away," she said. "How soon can you start?"

"As soon as you need me to!" I replied. Even though it would be a quick transition, I decided to go for it. I believed God was asking me to take a step of faith and move to North Carolina; out of my comfort zone, and out of the pit of despair.

The Holy Spirit was refueling my purpose. Although the road ahead was unclear, I knew I had to press the gas pedal *before* fear had a chance to stall my heart, so I packed up my bags and headed south. I prayed all the way that God would provide housing for me. I stayed at a cheap hotel my first night in Charlotte and went to work the very next day. I had money for three nights in a hotel, but nothing after that. I realize it might sound impulsive to move to a city with no place to live. Yet I knew I could no longer stay where I was. I felt compelled to move and steer into the unknown. God was navigating me in a new direction and filling my tank for the journey after a long emotional detour.

The last night at the hotel, I went to the lobby and searched online for a place to live. That's when I received a message on social media from someone named Greg, who was a friend of a friend of a friend. Greg said he'd heard I was looking for a place to live and that he and his wife were renting space in the apartment next to their home. Turns out, someone I knew mentioned to Greg that I was moving.

I told Greg I would stop by that night to see the space. The apartment was just what I was looking for. The only problem was the rent. They were asking for way more than I could afford per month, and there was no way I could pay it. Sadly, I told Greg thanks for the offer, but I could not afford the rent. "Well, what *can* you afford?" he asked me.

"I just started working and haven't even received my first paycheck yet. Probably only half of what you're asking."

"Well then, it's yours." he replied. Talk about a divine connection!

Greg's generosity helped top off my fuel tank and accelerate me toward my purpose. When God brought me through that experience, I wasn't the same person who went into it. The image of Christ had been branded on my heart in a way that only fiery trials can brand you.

God wants His character to be shaped and formed in our hearts, and He does this through alternating periods of heartbreak and healing in our lives. He will, without a doubt, make you steadfast, strong, and resilient as you endure hardship and persist toward your purpose.

Life Lesson

Stigma can't halt God's purpose for your life. He will refill your tank and refuel your heart as you allow Him to navigate you in the right direction. Never let the shame of stigma stop you in your tracks.

Shame-Stopping Scripture: "He brought me up also out of a horrible pit, out of the miry clay, and set my feet upon a rock, and established my goings. And he hath put a new song in my mouth, even praise unto our God: many shall see it, and fear, and shall trust in the LORD" (Psalm 40: 2–3, KJV). Write down the vision you see for yourself as you overcome your season of stigma and setbacks.

____

____

____

____

____

____

____

____

HeartBRAKE #7
The Shame of Toxic Cycles

Have you ever thought you were close to your destination, only to realize you've been driving around in circles? Most of us have had this experience at one time or another. Perhaps your GPS failed, or you misread the instructions and couldn't find the exact location. As a result, you unknowingly drove around and around, searching for a way to get to where you were going. If you've ever experienced this, you understand the frustration of not knowing how to reach your destination. That's how it feels when you're stuck in a toxic relationship cycle. You're wondering, *How will I ever get out of this?*

What makes a cycle toxic? A toxic cycle is one that depletes you emotionally, mentally, and spiritually over time. It changes you. It strips you of joy, steals your peace, and turns you into someone you don't really want to be. It's a pattern that's not healthy for your heart to keep repeating, yet you do it anyway, endlessly going in circles, looking for a way out. Oh, you might be smiling on the outside, showing the world what they want to see. But inside you're suffering in silence. I know this kind of pain well—the kind of pain that turns to shame the more you hide what's really going on.

Perhaps it's a relationship you just can't leave. Or you leave and go back. Again. And again. And again. Yes, I've been there too. You can't change the cycle, so you stop talking about it to others, thinking they are probably sick of hearing about it. The pain goes on and on and on.

What is the fuel for toxic cycles? It's called ambivalence. You choose one option and vow, *I'm going to leave if things don't change soon.* You're sure it's the right choice. You are determined to walk away. Only to reconsider your decision a few days later, thinking, *Maybe I'll stick things out.* You become perpetually indecisive, which only feeds the cycle of ambivalence even more.

Ambivalence is the mental angst that comes from going back and forth about something, and never reaching a conclusion you stick with. Sometimes indecisiveness goes on for so long it becomes your new normal, habitual—the only thing you know how to do. You can't make a change long enough to create the true freedom you long for. So you stay in a familiar cycle, and the dynamic continues to be unhealthy. When you try to leave the situation, you find yourself going back to it once again. The toxicity keeps repeating itself like a vicious vortex. There's no shame like the shame of a repetitive, toxic cycle that fuels unending ambivalent actions—or often, inactions.

A good definition of ambivalence is found in the book of James. In Chapter One of this book, an ambivalent person is described as a "double-minded man." James says this kind of person (one who is double-minded or ambivalent) is "unstable in all his ways" (James 1:8). James uses an ocean metaphor to give us an example of what ambivalence feels like. He says it's "like a wave of the sea driven and tossed by the wind" (James 1:6). Just as driving around in circles is disorienting, ambivalence in decision-making is confusing. An ambivalent person lacks enough fuel in their rocket booster to propel them forward into lasting change. I know what that's like, particularly when the decision to be made will drastically alter your life. For me, ambivalence in one area tends to spill over into others. The lack of decision-making in one area leaks into the next area of life, and so on.

One ambivalent time in my life I was struggling to decide which direction to take after being in a ten-year relationship with someone. It was by far one of the most difficult cycles I've ever had to break. In this case, the person wasn't toxic, but the cycle itself was unhealthy because over time it began to suffocate the deepest desires of my heart. Somewhere, at some point, those desires seemed to have smoldered out along the way, and there I was driving in circles year after year—never quite reaching a destination. I just couldn't break *free.*

Have you ever experienced the shame of a toxic cycle you can't break free from? Maybe you're trying to decide whether you should stay with someone for the long haul. Maybe they want to marry you, but you're not sure about making a lifelong commitment to them. Or vice versa. You keep trying to make it work. You keep trying to make things fit together and line up a certain way. You may be in a relationship for a very long time, for years even, wondering if you should end the relationship with this person or stay with them. What once flowed so smoothly now feels like striving and strain. It used to be easy, but now it feels complicated and messy, and you're wondering if you should hold out hope for things to change, or just move on. *But you cannot commit to a* *decision.* The back and forth continues until a toxic cycle is formed that is ever-so-hard to break.

If the relationship is abusive or neglectful, it poses additional challenges. You've grown accustomed to the up and down roller coaster ride. You've learned to tolerate the unending back and forth cycle of shame. You've done it so long that you accept it as your new normal. You've settled for a lack of fulfillment and happiness because you've convinced yourself "the devil you know is better than the devil you don't." Before you realize it, you're in a toxic comfort zone. Yes, even comfort zones can become toxic when they are prolonged and paralyzing.

On the flip side of staying too long, I have also found myself too isolated, barricaded behind walls I put up toward the opposite sex because I feared being rejected. I have also feared getting it wrong again or any number of other complications that might arise. I have lived in, and nurtured, toxic comfort zones of fear, unsure how to let my walls down and be open to love again—sometimes wondering if I even wanted to. After a string of messy break-ups, it's easy to get discouraged and think romantic love might not be a possibility for you. Every one of your insecurities rises to the surface. You start to wonder if you're even capable of navigating a romantic relationship with someone. It can be heartbreaking to experience the same repeating cycles and toxic patterns over and over. You wonder, *How do I maintain hope that I can ever have a healthy, loving relationship?*

After another stint in counseling to work through the walls I built around my heart, I began identifying the root of my own toxic patterns and relationship cycles. Through deeper attachment work, I learned that

I often attract either avoidant types or reckless types. My therapist helped me understand the factors that played a part in this attraction. It can be beneficial to look closely at relationship patterns to identify what kind of person you attract that's unhealthy, which parts of your heart are unhealthy, and why the cycle continues. At this point in life, I was ready for a new approach. As I reflected upon my previous dating patterns, I realized I had always waited for the guy to determine what *he* wanted, and then conformed to *his* game plan rather than taking an assertive role in the process myself. *Maybe I've been shortchanging myself,* I thought.

I sensed the time had come to be open to a different approach, one in which I could practice developing new patterns instead of reverting to old ones, so I began to consider online dating. This big step out of my "traditional dating comfort zone" stirred up a familiar feeling of fear inside me. The idea of breaking out of a comfort zone, however, would soon override the fear. My openness to a new approach started when I saw a friend's wedding pictures posted on social media. In the caption, my friend referenced "meeting and marrying my husband in a non-traditional way."

I was intrigued, and to be honest, somewhat jealous. I once heard someone say that jealousy gives us helpful information about what we desire in life. I believe this statement is true. Jealousy can help us know what kind of life we desire. Yet being consumed with jealousy is *not* helpful. Without keeping it in check, jealousy will lead to thoughts of comparison, covetousness, and self-pity—just to name a few. So I prayed, *Instead of being jealous, what I can learn from this situation, God?* When I called my friend to congratulate her, I asked her how she and her husband met. She told me that the non-traditional approach she took, which led to meeting her husband, was hiring a dating coach. A dating coach? *How timely,* I thought. *I was just considering alternative ways of meeting someone and now she mentions this coaching idea to me.* Since I was determined to stop driving around in circles and open myself up to doing things differently, I decided to try her approach. After our conversation, I emailed a dating coach and gave it a try.

My coach, Amy, didn't waste any time. She quickly gave me a reality check about my limited dating perspective, which contradicted almost everything I had been taught, told, or believed about dating. She pointed out how people in our culture are getting married later in life (or not getting married at all) because they are often stuck in negative or stagnant ways of thinking, as well as familiar patterns of behavior. Her philosophy was simple: learn what's not working in your dating life and then fix it by doing something different, even when it requires taking some radical steps. I knew she would push me (like a coach should) outside of my comfort zone—something I feared yet longed for at the same time.

As soon as I began stepping out in a new direction, ambivalence began to rear its ugly head. As I embraced the idea of joining a dating site, which was recommended by my coach, I realized my next decision was deciding which one. There were so many: *Match*, *eHarmony*, *Christian Mingle*, *Zoosk*, *Plenty of Fish*, *OkCupid*, *Hinge*, and countless others. Not to mention the abundance of personal matchmakers, eager to help you find the love of your life. Overwhelmed by the myriad choices, hesitation began to slow me down. Then it hit me. Maybe what was really stopping me was not the fear of change but the fear of *failure*. My mind was trying to convince me that if I didn't do anything at all, I wouldn't have any regrets—like signing up for the wrong dating site.

I'm not suggesting the way out of a toxic cycle or comfort zone is through online dating. Nor am I promising this method is how you will find your mate. Everyone's path is different. What I *am* saying is that taking a bold step in a new direction can break the cycle of ambivalence. For me, during this time of my life, the solution was to try a new process.

The root of all ambivalence is hidden fear—that's what it boils down to. Most of the time, an ambivalent heart indicates you are afraid of making a mistake and going down the wrong path. You fear regret. You dread rejection. You'd rather play it safe. You don't trust yourself to make good decisions, or trust God to work everything out in the end. The Book of James gives good advice on how to get out of the trap of ambivalence. "If any of you lacks wisdom, let him ask of God, who gives to all liberally and without reproach, and it will be given to him" (James 1:5).

You may be thinking, *I do ask God, but I still don't know what to do.* That's when verse six of the same chapter further encourages us to: "Ask in *faith*" (James 1:6). These verses mean that you can ask God, while at the same time trusting and believing that whether you get clear direction or not, you can still make decisions knowing that He's intimately involved in your process, as well as the outcome. Asking in faith, while decisively acting, will prevent you from continuously driving around in circles. *When you take the first step, you close the door on ambivalence and open the door of possibilities.* When you open the door of possibilities while trusting God's guidance, you can live life full of faith instead of fear.

As you continue practicing the skill of asking, trusting, and deciding, you will strengthen your decision-making muscles. I realize there are specific times in life, when deep down, you sense God is asking you to wait on Him and not take matters into your own hands. For example, perhaps you are separated from your spouse but not legally divorced. You are eager to move on, yet know in your heart God wants you to wait until one chapter of your life closes before starting the next chapter. These are the times you need to be still for a while. On the other hand, when there is nothing but fear itself holding you back, and you have a pattern of being scared to move to the left or the right, staying still for too long is a poor strategy for navigating through life. God wants you to step out in faith and trust Him. The verses in James I just shared is where I go when I need to get out of the passenger seat of ambivalence and into the driver's seat of faith.

As I moved forward with the online dating process, the voice of fear whispered that I was taking the wrong step. Secretly I wondered if the internet approach somehow meant I wasn't capable of meeting someone in person. Soon I started thinking I wasn't trusting divine providence to unfold in this area of my life. However, instead of following my fear, I decided to pray, act, and trust that God would work all things together for my good, like James 1:6 and Romans 8:28 promise. Sure enough, once I pushed through my indecisiveness, I experienced a *shift.* I was no longer vacillating, I was taking steps forward—and that felt great.

An insightful supervisor once told me, "The *process* you go through is more important than the *outcome.*" I have recalled this advice many times in my life. I don't always get the outcome I want when I walk by faith, but God's process *in me* is far more valuable than anything He has *for me.* Jesus wants us to stop driving around in circles of ambivalence and move forward so we can grow in Him. If we remain indecisive and double-minded, it's difficult for God to guide us and grow us up because we aren't taking any steps.

Have you ever tried to coax a toddler to begin walking? What do you do? You steady her hands and arms and then step back and call her toward you. As she takes those first few steps, you are there to catch her when she falls. That's what God does for us. However, sometimes we are so paralyzed by the *what ifs* that we aren't willing to take a step and try something new. We are fixated on God doing something one specific way, and we are unwilling to move in a new direction. Moving away from ambivalence will force us to change and grow.

Don't you want to take steps of faith so God can catch your hands and lead you? Taking steps of faith means stepping away from an old mindset or pattern so you can embrace new experiences in life.

As I entered the uncharted territory of online dating, I wasn't sure if that was the way I would meet a potential partner. I didn't know if it would produce the kind of outcome I wanted at all. What I did know, however, was that God put the desire for a mate in my heart, and it was okay for me to move toward this desire instead of remaining stuck in fear. As I left the land of ambivalence, I realized that going online was *not* a lack of trust that God would provide a mate if that was His will. I was simply leaving the land of complacency and steering in a new direction, while believing my Heavenly Father would guide me. I kept going on terrain I had never traveled before, trusting Christ to lead the way.

My online experience was not without its share of speed bumps. I received some off-the-wall messages from some questionable characters, leading me to think, *Maybe this is not for me.* But I resisted the temptation to retreat in defeat and stayed put instead. I was determined to give the experience a solid try. I didn't dive into it with the expectation that I would meet my husband. I had faith without forcing outcomes. I continued to remind myself the journey was a learning experience that was more about me growing through the process than producing results. God was shaping me into His image through this adventure by teaching me to walk by faith while trusting His sovereign plans. After trying the online dating approach for awhile, it started to become an enjoyable experience. I became more confident in myself and what I was looking for in a guy than I'd been in the past. I had the Holy Spirit as my navigator, and I knew this non-traditional dating approach would help me grow out of the comfort zone I'd stayed in for far too long.

Many situations have the potential to create ambivalence and cause us to drive longer than necessary in circles as we consider decisions about dating, marriage, children, career changes, or moving. When it comes to setting boundaries with loved ones we may repeat any number of patterns too long until they become toxic. But we don't have to stay in a place of shame and fear. God often strategically places people in our lives to help us navigate through these places of stuckness.

Looking back, I can think of many times when I felt unsure about a situation and someone came along at just the right time to help me. Someone was there to "hold up my arms," like Aaron did for Moses. A person was there to say just the right thing at the right time to help me move forward in my process. Let's revisit this story about Moses and

Aaron. In chapter 17 of Exodus, Moses was called by God to lead Israel into battle. God told Moses that when he (Moses) held up the rod, God would cause Israel to prevail over their enemies. However, the battle was long and Moses was weary. Have you ever felt weary from the battle of toxic cycles and patterns that seem impossible to change?

What battle have you fought for a long time that feels too hard to fight anymore? We can't fight alone. Exodus 17:12 says, "Moses' hands became heavy…and Aaron and Hur supported his hands." God will send people to hold up your hands, *or your heart,* or whatever you need them to hold, as you try to change stagnant situations. I simply can't encourage you enough—you don't have to stay in a place of shame regarding a pattern that seems impossible to change. Others can help. It may be a life coach, a counselor, a friend, a pastor, or a random stranger who gives you words of wisdom and encouragement at just the right time. I have experienced this kind of support time and time again. Sometimes I didn't recognize it in the moment because I was so focused on fighting the battle. Even now, as I reflect on how I got through several difficult ambivalent times, a person usually comes to mind who helped me along the way, just as Aaron did for Moses. God will do the same thing for you, if you let Him.

Did I meet my special someone online? No I didn't, but I *did* meet some very interesting people along the way and learned much about myself in the process. Being brave and trying something new catapulted me out of ambivalence and into freedom.

Be on the lookout for an Aaron to help you. Be assured that you *can* make decisions in faith, focusing on the beauty of God's process within you, rather than the outcome ahead of you. Remember, steering away from toxic cycles will *empower* you to grow in productive ways.

Life Lesson

To leave toxic cycles behind and stop driving around in circles, take a step in a new direction. Then, trust God wholeheartedly to guide your path and steer you back on course if you veer off track.

Shame-Stopping Scripture: The Bible says a double-minded man is "unstable in all his ways" (James 1:8). How do you see yourself driving away from ambivalence towards solid decision-making in your life?

____

____

____

____

____

____

____

____

HeartBRAKE #8
The Shame of Unrequited Love

Unexpected delays can turn a short, well-mapped-out road trip into an endless, unfamiliar journey. Does your life have you on a path you didn't expect, with winding roads that keep you from reaching your destination? Sometimes we make decisions that, in retrospect, we aren't sure were the best ones, and the effects of those choices can be frustrating.

One kind of heartbreak shame that is difficult to endure is unrequited love. You love someone who doesn't love you back the same way you love them. You may wait, hope, and pray for affection from the person you love, yet there seems to be no change in how they feel or how they treat you.

You long for the desires of your heart to be fulfilled with *this* person, but before you know it, one year turns into two, or five, or maybe even ten or more. You've tried to find freedom from the situation. Perhaps you've even been in counseling for a long time. You want relief from the regrets and unmet desires you replay over and over in your mind. You want a remedy for the deep pain within your heart that comes from loving someone who can't—or won't—love you back.

I once worked with one woman who was in love with a man for ten years who didn't love her back the same way she loved him. They met in college, and he seemed to show interest in her initially. She perceived his kind words as flirtations. She mistook his sweet smile for a secret crush, and his glances her way as hints that he liked her as more than a friend. They even hung out together on occasion. Before long she was hooked. She desperately wanted more from him, but he never gave her the true love her heart deeply longed for. Yet, she could *not* break free. She came to me full of shame for loving him for so long and feeling foolish because of it. She stopped talking to her friends about it because deep down she just knew they wouldn't understand.

Whenever you are seeking healing from unrequited love and its related heartbreak shame, it takes perseverance. Perseverance is what happens when you train your mind, body, and emotions to endure a particular process *until* you experience a breakthrough, shift, or turn in a different direction. It takes self-control to persevere. It requires cross-country road trip kind of faith. It's what Jesus learned to do during His own uphill battle to the cross until He was finally set free from His earthly limitations. "He learned obedience by the things which He suffered" (Hebrews 5:8).

Here's a practical example to illustrate this spiritual principle. The year I decided to run my first marathon, I didn't know what the commitment would entail. As I began to investigate what training for the race would involve, I became more aware of the price I would have to pay to prepare for this monumental feat. I reviewed my training schedule for the coming several months and considered the hours of prep time. I knew I was in for a cross-country drive, not a quick road trip! Marathoners run for 26.2 miles. However, our bodies only store twenty miles' worth of glycogen, the glucose your body needs to produce energy.

As I progressed with the training program, one question remained: *What happens after mile twenty? How will I finish the race without the internal supply of energy I need?* I learned from my trainer that my body would need to access energy from other sources, such as fat cells and carbohydrates, to keep running.

Much like marathon training, at certain times in life we must discipline our minds and bodies to endure a particular trial after we have run out of the strength it takes to keep going. You can't take a shortcut. There is no detour around the struggle. You must press *through* it. Bear up under it. You need to walk a path of suffering until you get to the other side of it. And when you run out of fuel, you need to tap into a greater resource, Jesus, to withstand the process until it is complete.

Your mind wants to start searching for answers, an escape, when it gets incredibly hard to keep running. Many times, there is no explanation for what you're going through when it's happening. It's only after the trial that you gain understanding—sometimes right after it, sometimes a long time after it—and sometimes you never get a full understanding of why you went through what you went through.

Much of the work I do in counseling is with people who are on the long-distance road trips of life. Marriage is a great example of a cross-country drive, versus a short road trip. Most relationships in our culture begin with a romantic high as the foundation for the union. Think back to when you first met your husband, wife, boyfriend, or girlfriend, and reflect upon the early stages of your relationship. It was most likely filled with chemistry, romance, laughter, late night calls, long dates, gifts, gab, and *more romance!*

One of the most common heartbreaks people experience is the disillusionment that comes from long-term commitment. A phrase I hear often is, "Things turned out much differently than I expected in our relationship—I didn't sign up for this." Other phrases include: "He doesn't love me like he used to" and "He or she has changed so much; I don't know if I'm in love with him/her anymore." Which often leads to, "Maybe I made a mistake when I married him." Perhaps your relationship started out with lots of passion and now there is barely a flicker of attraction. How do you tell your partner you aren't attracted to them anymore? *Should* you even tell them? There can be many shameful feelings involved when desire has been drained from your heart and you don't know what to do.

If you know the pain and disappointment of a long-term relationship that's gone south, you're not alone. Maybe you've wrestled with the confusion that comes from not knowing if you love your spouse anymore, or if they love you, for years. You may have even experienced the devastating effects of an affair, the distress of a partner's chronic depression or anxiety, the challenges of parenting conflicts, the loss of a child, work addiction, sex addiction, the letdown of falling out of love, the loneliness of growing apart, the hurt of being misunderstood, or other issues. The list goes on and on. By the time people come in for counseling, if they make it there at all, one or both of them are burned out from the continual disappointments they've experienced along the way. Many couples have checked out of the relationship and are hanging on by a thread.

One technique I introduce to couples in distress is called *Imago Therapy*. This method was developed by therapist Harville Hendrix and has been used to help countless couples find healing. Hendrix studied thousands of relationships and came to some interesting conclusions. He examined the effects that attraction has on the brain from the early stages of a connection until the later stages of a relationship.

When couples first meet, there is usually an intense attraction. Chemicals such as oxytocin and dopamine fire continuously in the brain, which bonds couples together and makes them feel like they are on a love high. Studies show that after one to two years, these chemicals stop firing as rapidly, and the love high starts to plateau. This leveling off is when people feel as though they have fallen *out* of love or hit a romantic roadblock. Quarreling replaces cuddling. Negative characteristics are seen more readily than positive ones, and discouragement about staying committed sets in.

Hendrix believes that while attraction and chemistry dominate the early stages of a relationship, a deeper, subconscious attraction rules the latter stages of a relationship. This subconscious attraction is a composite of the negative and positive traits of each person's primary caregivers. In other words, initially we are attracted to the positive traits of our partner: the loving, kind, captivating aspects of their personality. However, after the chemicals subside, the more negative traits appear, making one think they married the wrong person or have fallen out of love. So why do people scramble to exit the relationship, or stoically stay in stalemate? *Imago Theory* argues it's because this person has unhealed childhood pain that they expect their partner to fix.[4]

For example, let's say that your father was distant, unaffectionate, and un-affirming. You might marry someone who is initially close and connected to you, but after some time, they gradually become detached and seem to care more about other things than about you. *What went wrong?* you wonder. You feel alone in the relationship, constantly vying for your partner's attention. Over time, you begin to withdraw from them, feeling trapped inside a miserable, lonely marriage. Deep down, you want your partner to be there for you like your father never was.

Perhaps you married someone like your mother; someone who was critical, controlling, and never satisfied, reminiscent of the Prince song, "When Doves Cry." In the beginning, your partner seemed so caring and concerned, always encouraging you and cheering you on. But after a while, the concern turned to control, and you realize your spouse is different than you thought. They are moody and sullen instead of motivating and sincere. You tell yourself things will change, yet constantly wonder if they ever will.

What went wrong? you wonder.

What went wrong is what happens to most couples. You were attracted to (consciously drawn to) the positive characteristics of your partner, only to later discover you were also attracted to (subconsciously drawn to) their negative traits. In a frantic attempt to heal unfinished business from childhood, you try to change the other person. In the later stages of a relationship, when the subconscious attraction is dominant, most people find themselves living unhappily ever after. Or they desperately search for a way out. At times, one or both partners may have a physical or emotional affair to get their needs met from someone other than their spouse. Hendrix explains that it takes work to stay happily married, instead of exiting or sabotaging the relationship.

It can be distressing, disappointing, and heartbreaking to wake up every day to a painful, loveless relationship. One couple I worked with described feeling chronically alone in their marriage. The husband used a metaphor to explain that he wasn't sure how to go from an island (a solitary place) to the mainland (a trusting partnership) with his mate again. One woman described the pain of living with her husband as he battled sexual addiction. She felt like the object of his lust, always wondering if he was comparing her to the women in the pornography he viewed. After working with this woman over time, I realized she was displaying the same characteristics of someone who had been traumatized or abused. I began to study this topic and found that many people who are in a relationship with someone who has a sex addiction display these traits. Working with her and others led me to this conclusion: Even though pornography is culturally acceptable in many people's eyes, I believe the use of porn by one person without their spouse's knowledge is a form of infidelity, and repeated infidelity in a relationship is a form of abuse.

In addition to infidelity, many other forms of abuse can take place in relationships, and it's common for the person being abused to rationalize the abuser's behavior by blaming it on themselves or dismissing it completely. However, abuse doesn't go away on its own. At some point it must be acknowledged, faced, and dealt with. With the right kind of counseling and perseverance, you *can* face it and deal with it. Yet when abuse is repetitive in your relationship or marriage, you don't have to deal with it and stay in it for the long haul. You aren't required to take this kind of road trip in life.

Abuse takes the following forms: emotional, verbal, physical, sexual, spiritual, and mental. Another form of abuse, which may encompass some of the forms of abuse I just mentioned, has gained much attention recently—narcissistic abuse.

Emotional abuse includes manipulation, mental control, intimidation, and mind games such as lying, cheating, and gaslighting.

Verbal abuse is any form of shouting, belittling, name-calling, put downs or other attempts to make you feel insecure about yourself.

Physical abuse is harmful or hurtful touch, such as pushing, punching, pinching, choking, or slapping.

Sexual violence, also called sexual abuse, is according to the Center for Family Justice, "any sexual contact or behavior that happens without your consent. Other names used for sexual abuse include: rape and sexual assault."[5]

Spiritual abuse is a form of mental and psychological manipulation, used by someone who wants to control another person's decision making and autonomy. For example, the abusive person might emphasize strict adherence to rules, and use shame to force another to be "obedient" to them. A spiritually abusive person will use the name of God, or specific scriptures, to coerce or dominate another for their own benefit. Spiritual abuse can happen in any church or denomination.

Mental abuse includes one person controlling the other, for example, dictating: who the other one talks to, what they wear or where they go. Mental abuse can also occur within a marriage and encompasses; engaging in emotional or physical affairs, manipulating your spouse, and using intimidating behaviors, such as towering over them, yelling in their face, blocking their exit, and forcing them to listen.

Another kind of abuse that's on the rise is narcissistic abuse, which I talk about in Chapter 11. I am encountering this kind of abuse more and more in my line of work. I also experienced it personally with a man I once dated. Narcissistic abuse is subtle and insidious. Abusers choose their victims, usually empaths, people who are kind and nurturing, to confuse and control for their own gain.

No one should endure any kind of abuse. Yet many people do endure it because of how hard it can be to leave a relationship. You feel like a quitter. Or you're afraid to be alone. There are different variables you aren't sure how to navigate through. It's especially difficult when you've been with the other person for a very long time. *True love only happens once in a lifetime; this is my soul mate,* you tell yourself. Yet I assure you, *true* soul mates don't want to hurt you. They don't want you to suffer. Yes, suffering happens in relationships when life throws curveballs, but if someone is causing you suffering intentionally, that's not a soul mate.

I know it's hard to let go, but is it worth staying in a relationship where you feel constant turmoil? Is it worth giving up yourself for someone who is mistreating you? Give yourself permission to surrender the person to God and to live your life. Live life the way you were born to, the way you were created to, the way you desire to, and *the way God intended you to.* You weren't made to live in fear, with low self-esteem, or with another person's addiction or rage issues controlling and ruling your life. It's not worth it. *Loving* might mean *leaving.* Sometimes the most loving thing you can do is to leave someone, thus ending the destructive cycle you've both been trapped in. Ye*s,* you get to decide what is best for you and what's not. And at the right time, I know you'll make the decision that's best for you.

Please talk to a trusted friend or counselor if you think you have been, or are being, physically, emotionally, or sexually abused in any way. Many times abuse causes a deep root of shame in your soul. You blame yourself for things that were never your fault. You may think you are trapped. You may think you will never get over it or get out of it. You may think it's the bed you made, so you have to lie in it, but that's not true. You *can* get out. You may think what's happening is love. But it's *not* love. It's a toxic cycle that only *feels* like love. *Dear friend, abusive behavior is* ***never*** *love.*

If there is no abuse, yet your marriage is desperately unsatisfying and disappointing, that's another story. Perhaps you're on a cross-country drive in a vehicle that needs a tune-up before it can continue any further. Once you understand your *Imago* (your subconscious attraction) you can begin working on understanding how your childhood wounds are triggered in your relationship and what you can do to heal those wounds. It may be beneficial for you to think about marriage counseling, specifically with someone who is trained in couple's therapy and can help you move toward a place of healing and restoration in your relationship.

It is possible to thrive in your marriage, but it may require work and perseverance before moving to the next level of satisfaction. You don't have to settle for living as roommates or resign to getting divorced. If you are willing to acknowledge the pain, instead of anesthetizing it, and take the necessary steps towards healing, there *is* hope for you. I have seen many couples who were heading toward divorce, and instead, they found healing through the counseling process. They chose to do the hard work necessary to change their relationship. Sometimes no matter how hard you try, divorce is inevitable, but it doesn't have to be the end of your story! You *can* heal from the pain and live free of shame.

I, too, have experienced the pain of unrequited love when it comes to relationships. I've been in several committed relationships that went on for long periods of time—longer than they should have. I've always been a loyal person, someone who is a friend to the end. I'm willing to walk with you through the valleys of despair and stay by your side until you come through the tough places of life. That's why I love counseling. I love journeying with others through hardship and seeing them come out healthier and happier on the other side.

Although loyalty is a strength, it can also be a weakness when it involves an unhealthy devotion to someone who's not as devoted to you. Have you experienced this kind of heartbreak? This kind of "love" burns up your battery and uses all your gas without offering much in return. This kind of love flattens your tires and eats away at your engine. It's exhausting to love someone in this way.

So how do you know when to remain on the relationship road and when to cut the trip short? There's not a black-and-white answer for this dilemma. Often, it requires prayer and wise counsel. There are times in life when we need to persevere. Yet there are also times when we need to give ourselves permission to walk away; times when we are being used or abused, or when we are codependent, enmeshed, or running on empty. Times when we have completely depleted our tank and need to let go in order to grow.

In situations like these, praying the Serenity Prayer can be helpful.

God, grant me the serenity to ACCEPT the things I cannot change,
the courage to CHANGE the things I can,
and the wisdom to KNOW the difference.

The answer doesn't always come easily, even when you pray. Sometimes it's a process of trial and error until you figure it out. There are no quick fixes, or one-size-fits-all spiritual answers. I've heard expressions such as "If God wants you to do_______, He will give you peace" or "You will know you are doing the right thing because God will provide for you." I can say from experience, peace or provision may not come—at least not how you may think. There have been times when God prompted me to do something, and all I felt was fear, not peace. There have also been times when I've had to step out in faith when there was no provision in sight, but I knew it was right.

Do you think Jesus had peace before He went to the cross? The Bible tells us He was sweating drops of blood. That indicates great suffering and mental anguish. On the way to His crucifixion, Jesus knew it was the will of God. But He certainly didn't have a warm fuzzy feeling about it. It was a sacrificial act of obedience. Just as the Holy Spirit was with Jesus, He will be with you, giving you wisdom in your discernment process. He will not leave you or forsake you (Hebrews 13:5). He will show you the way to go (Isaiah 30:21).

Another way to determine if you should stay the course or change direction is through fasting. Fasting is a way to suppress the appetites of the flesh to hear the voice of the Spirit. The Bible offers different kinds and examples of fasts. One of my favorite fasts is called the Daniel Fast, found in the book of Daniel, Chapter One. Daniel chose to abstain from the King's meat and eat only vegetables for a specific amount of time. "Prove thy servants, I beseech thee, ten days; and let them give us pulse to eat, and water to drink" (Daniel 1:12, KJV). Some scholars define "pulse" as fruit and vegetables. Other descriptions include whole grains such as rice and millet. Either way, your diet is only one component of fasting. Food shouldn't be your primary focus. Instead, spending time with God in prayer and reading His Word are of primary importance.

During a fast, sometimes prayer comes easily and you're in sync with the Spirit. Other times, you'll feel distracted and restless. You may have committed to abstaining from sweets during your fast, yet are caught off guard when a coworker brings donuts to work, so you have one. Maybe you've decided to give up social media, then find yourself logging onto your account out of impulse. If that happens, don't be hard on yourself by focusing on what you didn't do right. The quicker you pick yourself up and start again, the better off you'll feel. It's easy to succumb to guilt-ridden thoughts, like you shouldn't have eaten that, or watched this, or done that. Fasting is hard. It takes a tremendous amount of discipline and self-control to do it, and you're not perfect. Even experienced fasters give in to their own flesh at times.

Paul said, "For what I am doing, I do not understand. For what I will to do, that I do not practice; but what I hate, that I do" (Romans 7:15). Paul spent an entire chapter explaining the raging war between the flesh and the spirit. Jesus Himself experienced the temptation to eat during a fast when the devil suggested that He "command that these stones become bread" (Matthew 4:3). If you begin your fast knowing you *will* be tempted, it won't catch you off guard or knock you off course when it happens. The most important thing you can do is to simply *start again* and *refocus* on the purpose of your fast.

God's desire is not for you to spend lots of energy thinking about what you did or didn't do right, but rather to focus on discovering what He wants to *show* you or *say* to you during this time. The Prophet Isaiah says, "*Is* this not the fast that I have chosen: To loose the bonds of wickedness, To undo the heavy burdens, To let the oppressed go free, And that you break every yoke?" (Isaiah 58:6).

Here, God emphasizes fighting for justice and advocating for the oppressed, not holing up in a room somewhere thinking about what you are or aren't eating. God will be faithful to you during your fast.

Isaiah 58:8–12 (NKJV) shares the blessings of fasting…

> Then your light shall break forth like the morning, Your healing shall spring forth speedily, And your righteousness shall go before you; the glory of the LORD shall be your rear guard. Then you shall call, and the LORD will answer; you shall cry, and He will say, 'Here I *am.*' If you take away the yoke from your midst, the pointing of the finger, and speaking wickedness, *If* you extend your soul to the hungry and satisfy the afflicted soul, Then your light shall dawn in the darkness, And your darkness shall *be* as the noonday. The LORD will guide you continually, And satisfy your soul in drought, and strengthen your bones; you shall be like a watered garden, and like a spring of water, whose

> waters do not fail. Those from among you Shall build the old waste places; You shall raise up the foundations of many generations; And you shall be called the Repairer of the Breach, the Restorer of Streets to Dwell In.

The above passage makes it clear that fasting and prayer have multiple rewards. Look at each verse and notice the benefits attached to each one. God longs to provide for you in many ways, whether it's restored health, renewed hope in His promises, or strength in the waiting process. God is always with you. Whether He gives a direct answer to your prayers, or the strength for a deeper surrender to His plans, changes do occur through fasting and prayer.

One time in my life, I was in a difficult place and struggling to find peace. I was stuck in the shame cycle of another heartbreaking relationship, and I felt forgotten by God. I was desperate for change and didn't know where to turn next, so I decided to go on a fast to get closer to Jesus and seek His will.

I reached out to several friends to tell them what I was going through. It was hard to be vulnerable; I'm naturally more comfortable being independent and figuring things out on my own. As a counselor and life coach, I've been trained to help others, and I rarely talk about my own problems. However, God brought me to a place of such humility that I had to cry out for help. I emailed five friends and said, "Please pray for me for the next twenty-one days in these specific areas. I really need your support."

Then I started one of my favorite books on fasting, *The Power of Fasting and Prayer*, by Marilyn Hickey. Marilyn talks about the purpose of fasting and shows you how to pick a theme and scripture for each day of your fast.[7] Since then, I've approached my fasting times much differently than I did in the early stages. Instead of being consumed with thoughts about what to eat or not eat, I learned to focus more on prayer and connecting with God throughout the day by meditating on specific scriptures. Marilyn's book teaches you how to fast in a practical way that's easy to understand.

When my fast concluded, God showed up in a tangible way. That's not always the case, but this time it was. He gave me the strength to let go of the relationship I was fasting about and break free from the shame that was keeping me stuck. My experience was Isaiah 58 in action, and I was so grateful for the blessings and power of His Word.

Another time in life when I was struggling with a particularly difficult decision, I decided to do a traditional Lenten fast. Those who fast during Lent typically do so for forty days. The number forty is significant in the Bible. The children of Israel wandered in the wilderness for forty years. I can relate. I have wandered in the wilderness for many seasons of my life. This time, I needed divine help getting out of the wilderness of winding roads all around me, so I decided to fast for a longer time. I want to mention here: *It's not the length of the fast that's important to God; it's the posture of your heart.* This time, I simply felt led to fast longer than usual. It was the same sensation I had when it was time to run my marathon—God was encouraging me to push past my limits and go deeper.

The nights leading up to the fast, I began having dreams—dreams that involved eating lots of pizza and ice cream. I would wake up in the morning nervous about starting the fast, thinking about what I would have to give up that day. It's normal to dream and think a lot about food when you're fasting, by the way. It is your flesh's response to dying to what it wants.

During this fast, there was daily scripture I prayed over myself and others. I focused on several themes—specific areas where I believed God would bring clarity, direction, or restoration. This time, something different happened during my prayer time with Jesus. I saw an image in my mind of ocean waves flowing in and out upon the shore. As I saw the vision, I sensed the words, "Just like the tides, I have things I want you to embrace right now, and other things I want you to let go of." Those words were the nudge I needed to make some necessary changes in my life. This example demonstrates the power of fasting and prayer.

Life Lesson

God will work on your behalf one way or the other, either by answering your prayers, giving you strength, or helping you rest in Him while you wait for change to come. I've also learned that unrequited and abusive love do not have to be endured. It's never too late to choose a different path and live life to the fullest. In due time, long-distance heartbreaking drives always yield God-given wisdom as we surrender our hearts and lives to Him.

HeartBRAKE #8

Shame-Stopping Scripture: "That your faith should not be in the wisdom of men but in the power of God" (1 Corinthians 2:5). What might God be asking you to endure? What might He want you to release from your life? Pray for the wisdom of God and then journal your thoughts here.

____

____

____

____

HeartBRAKE #9

The Shame of Holiday Heartbreak

For many singles, it's tough being alone during the holidays, and it's especially difficult to experience a breakup during this time. I have spent many holiday seasons as a single lady, and while I'd like to say I've always been single and satisfied, I confess I've spent quite a few holidays stuck in shame rather than free from it. I couldn't fully grasp the idea of how to be grateful, rather than disappointed, when others were hitched and I was flying solo to holiday hangouts.

With increased access to social media, I've spent ample time checking other people's relationship statuses and comparing their experiences to mine. If I'm not careful, I tend to regress to my inner five-year-old, who throws a tantrum when things don't go her way. It's easy to become discouraged when your life hasn't turned out the way you thought it would, romantically speaking. It's tempting to measure your life against other people's and think, *Where did I go wrong?* Especially during the holidays.

Why do holidays seem so much harder to navigate than regular days? One reason is that occasions like birthdays, Christmas, and New Year's represent the passing of time. Each holiday marks another year gone by, which can trigger reminders of previous heartbreaks and unfulfilled dreams. When you compare yourself to others, emotions such as jealousy, anger, and depression can rise to the surface, snuffing out your attempts to focus on the positive aspects of your life. Instead, you scroll through people's pictures with a skewed version of what's going right for them and wrong for you.

The holidays can also highlight family heartbreaks. When you put a bunch of people together with different personalities, desires, and expectations for how they want things to go, conflict is inevitable. When family patterns surface, you may feel confined to familiar feelings. If you're single during the holidays, it's normal to feel misunderstood, particularly when family asks why you're not dating anyone or when you're going to get married. It can be challenging to see all your friends with their spouses and children during the holidays while you're single, especially if you've had repeated relationship detours over time. It can be heartbreaking to see pictures of weddings and babies on social media while you're still longing for that part of your life to start. It's difficult to be happy for others who are thriving relationally, when it feels like God has forgotten about you. Shame can rise to the surface when you feel *unhappily unhitched* among family.

But how about if you *are* hitched during the holidays? Does this protect you from shame? Not necessarily. It's quite common to experience feelings of shame when you're secretly struggling with a dating or marital issues your family is unaware of. You may be trying to paint a picture of a happy relationship while crying behind closed doors.

One of the keys to breaking free from shame is learning to embrace contentment. While at first that may sound like a rather ridiculous suggestion, I assure you it is not. Contentment is a state of mind. It's not based upon what you have or don't have. It's possible to obtain whether you're single or married, whether you're experiencing hardship or abundance. In the Bible, Paul talks about times when he went without and times when he had plenty. In both circumstances, he learned to be content (Philippians 4:12–13). One might even infer from these verses that if contentment can be learned, so can discontentment. Being dissatisfied can also be experienced whether there's lack *or* abundance in your life. In other words, *without* material things you can be discontent, and *with* material things you can be discontent. Much of it is, as I said before, a state of mind (and heart).

Let's peek at a few holiday heartbreaks I've experienced, and from these experiences, glean insights about how to become free from shame and how to embrace contentment, like Paul did.

One heartbreaking Christmas, I was ultra-aware of my singleness. I wanted to be grateful for the invitations I'd received to join festive gatherings, but I didn't have it in me. That year the longing to be married and have a family of my own was particularly relentless. Instead of spending time with other people and their families, I decided to pair up with a few single friends and go to a festive function. *What was my secret wish?* I was secretly hoping I might meet someone at the party this year. Oh, I pretended I was satisfied on the outside, but internally my focus was elsewhere. I had this whole scenario mapped out in my mind that someone at the party would sweep me off my feet. Is it wrong to desire that? Of course not! It's great to be open to meeting someone romantically at an event. However, in this case, I was preoccupied. Preoccupied by fairy-tale fantasies instead of being content in the moment.

What did I learn that year? That fantasizing about future outcomes instead of living in the moment, does *not* lead to contentment. The holiday romance I was hoping for didn't happen that Christmas. Nope, my Prince Charming didn't sweep me off my feet that night like Jude Law did for Cameron Diaz in *The Holiday*. Trying to escape my current reality didn't work. Instead, the familiar feeling of discontentment enveloped me like a thick, winter snow. That old unwelcome friend had returned. Deep down, I knew being in a relationship wasn't the solution to the shame I felt about not having a party date, and I understood that unless I had a change of heart, I was headed for another heartbreaking holiday. *I need to learn contentment in spite of my circumstances, like Paul did,* I reminded myself.

But what was his secret?

At the party, I decided to talk to a good friend and mentor about it. "Charlene, have you learned how to be content, the way Paul talks about in the Bible?" I asked. Charlene paused for a moment and pondered. Then she answered, "I'm not totally there, but I have learned to be *more* content during the holiday season then I used to be." "Really? I asked. How?" Well," she replied, "I've experienced a lot of loss in my life, and when you go through enough disappointments, you learn how to let go of what you've lost and be grateful for what you have."

Charlene went on to share how she'd lost several people she loved dearly at an early age. She described how lonely the holidays became for her after they were gone, since their house had been where everyone gathered to celebrate. After they passed away, the rest of the family dispersed, and everything about the holiday season changed. "In the American culture, there is a big emphasis on being with family and getting gifts during Christmas," Charlene said, "but what about the people who don't have families, or the money to buy gifts?" Charlene told me that each year before the holidays, she takes time to grieve who and what she has lost in the past. Then, instead of focusing on what she doesn't have, she makes a conscious choice to appreciate what she does have.

"Thankfulness," I sighed. Deep down, I saw that thankfulness was one of the keys to contentment. Yet learning to be thankful can be a serious challenge. Being thankful for what you do have, *despite* what you don't have, takes grit and maturity.

Sometimes I genuinely *want* to be thankful, but I don't *feel* thankful. *Is thankfulness a feeling? Or is it a posture of the heart we need to cultivate despite our feelings?* As I pondered these thoughts, something occurred to me. Whether or not gratitude is something you *feel* isn't what's most important. What's most important is how you *express* it. So how do you express thankfulness?

I reflected on people who were thankful in the Bible, hoping I'd find an answer there. That's when the passage in John 4 came to mind. As I let this passage sink in, I had a thought—perhaps thankfulness is fostered in God's presence. Even if you don't *feel* grateful, you can develop a grateful heart as you spend time with the One who is the both the *source* of all good things and the *author* of gratitude. As you bring your unquenched, holiday heartbreak shame to Christ, He will satiate your thirst with His living water, the water of His Spirit. This kind of water is a gratitude supplier. This water produces a soul-satisfying, thirst-quenching kind of contentment like no other. This kind of life-giving water is found only in God's presence.

The woman in the book of John discovered gratitude when she met Jesus at the well, and was enraptured by Him. That's where He revealed the secret of contentment to her. It's where He taught her about the kind of satisfaction and gratitude that comes exclusively from knowing Him. She was broken-hearted, and Jesus knew it. She'd had five previous husbands, and the man she was currently with was not committed to her (John 4:16–18). After she was satisfied in God's presence, with His living water, she unashamedly ran into the city to invite others to experience the same joy and gratitude she'd found in Him. (John 4:28–30). If you're struggling with contentment, I invite you to read John 4 today and ask God to fill you with His presence in a way He's never done before. He longs to do so!

Birthdays are another time I'm in danger of discontentment. This emotion is usually because I set high expectations for myself to accomplish a certain goal by that time, only to be disappointed if it doesn't happen that way. Or, I swing in the opposite direction and tell myself "it's just another day," and I set my expectations extremely low to avoid being disappointed. Both these strategies breed dissatisfaction.

One heartbreaking birthday, I decided to travel overseas. I was desperate to escape the growing anxiety inside me as I approached turning thirty-nine. It was the last year of my thirties, and I was determined to escape the reality that some of my most important dreams were not yet accomplished. I felt the shame and disappointment from those unreached milestones, and my solution was to travel as far away as possible. In a matter of days, my bags were packed. Looking back, I can see a pattern of avoiding pain by running to other places to escape it. Funny enough, I always seem to find the very feelings I was running from greet me with open arms when I get there!

One year I decided to go to Central America as part of my escape plan. As the departure date approached, my apprehension increased as I tried to distract myself by planning something important to do to celebrate my birthday, which fell during my trip. Two different options sounded appealing—either a scenic drive to the beach or to a local rainforest with lush waterfalls. As the planning commenced, memories of heartbreak shame flooded my mind, and I scrambled to keep busy. I quickly made a list of the pros and cons of each possibility and asked my good friend and traveling partner Sabrina for her advice. "Why don't you do whatever would make you happy," she advised. I laughed to myself, thinking, *Yes, if I only knew what that was.* My biggest fear was that I would inevitably sabotage my happiness by choosing one activity, then upon arrival, wish I had chosen the other option.

Eventually, I decided to go with the rainforest excursion because it was closer to our living quarters and less expensive. I excitedly began entertaining thoughts of trekking through tropical terrain peppered with waterfalls and wonderfully exotic wildlife. After a short restless night's sleep the night before my birthday, my special day started with a lump in my throat and tears in my eyes as the number *thirty-nine* loomed in front of me bright and early that morning. The minute the day began, I started to regret how far away from home I was. I quickly got dressed, attempting to divert my attention to packing and planning for the day's activity. *Don't cry Kristin, don't cry,* I said to myself. *Be happy! It's your birthday!*

What a great time to celebrate God's goodness in your life this past year. To anchor my soul, I sketched out a list of all the things I was grateful for the year before.

Soon it was time for Sabrina and I to dash off to the bus station, ready for my birthday adventure. We made a quick stop in San Juan for avocados, bread, and plantains to bring on our trek through the tropical rainforest. We boarded the bus prepared for the adventure ahead.

On the bus ride, I noticed the sky becoming increasingly gray and dreary. *That's what you get for choosing the rainforest,* I mumbled to myself. Soon after, we were dropped off at the foot of a hill at our destination. Fifty feet ahead was a short climb to the entrance where an inviting-looking trail greeted us. *Okay, this isn't so bad*, I thought. Just as I began embracing contentment, however, the rain began. This was not a misty rain—it was coming down fast and furious. I pulled my jacket tightly around me as a sad, sullen, feeling crept into my heart. Why was I gripped with gloominess? After all it is a *rain* forest! What was I expecting?

Then it happened. That yucky feeling of heartbreak shame smothered me again, this time, like a sopping blanket covering me from head to toe. Memories of all the dating detours in my thirties, the unfulfilled dreams, the shame of getting older, and the feeling of being so far behind, began swirling in my mind. *Uh-oh, here we go again.*

As Sabrina and I trekked our way to the trail, the reality of my surroundings sunk in. This was going to be a very cold, gray, wet birthday. There I was, turning thirty-nine in a dark, dreary, rainforest. I pleaded with God to get me out of the funk I was slipping into. I tried to see the beauty in the heavy rain falling on the smooth Costa Rican plants. I tried and tried and *tried,* but I just couldn't make myself think positively. Within minutes, my mascara-stained face matched the dewy drops of the dark skies.

Hearing the sound of my whimpers, Sabrina turned back toward me. In her best cheerleading voice, she said, "Come over here, Kristin! Look at the amazing caterpillar on this rare plant!" She was doing everything she could to cheer me up, but it wasn't working—not because of her lack of effort. It wasn't working because of me. *The sadness was all inside of me.* That dreaded feeling of shame and sadness I flew hundreds of miles to escape, through heights and hills had managed to find me in the middle of a foreign land. It was the nagging nemesis called *discontentment*, the foe that steals your peace and tauntingly tempts you to despair, and then leaves you to fend for yourself. On that day I knew deep down, like I'd never known before, that a *place* can't cure pain. Only freedom from shame can do that.

After the Costa Rican birthday adventure, I began to wonder if it was a mistake to build my hopes up so much in my thirties. Why did I allow myself to get my hopes up so high? Why hope for things when they continually got sideswiped by unexpected detours and delays?

Although I don't know the exact formula for how much hope to have at any age, I *do* know that God's Word seems to want us to have hearts *full* of hope at any given time (Hebrews 6:19). Through many heartbreaking experiences, I have learned that the *kind* of hope God wants us to have is hope that is anchored in Christ—hope that is fixed on Him, founded on Him, and fastened upon Him—*not* on our ever-changing circumstances. Fixing our eyes on Him is *not* succumbing to unending heartache when things don't go as planned.

This is another key to overcoming shame. God wants us to maintain hope in Him and in His Word, *not* in things going our way. With new insight regarding hope, I managed to survive turning thirty-nine—maybe not as happily as I would've liked to, but better equipped with important lessons to be applied during future special occasions.

In addition to Christmas and birthdays, another holiday that can steer me towards shame is New Year's. Although this holiday can be filled with hope, expectation, and the promise of good things to come, it can also be a time of disappointment about what didn't happen the previous year. For many people, New Year's Day is a reminder of past regrets. One heartbreaking New Year's Day, I woke up feeling like I was in the same exact place as the year before. I felt stuck. Stagnant. Trapped in time. I didn't know how to pull myself out of the slump I was falling into. New Year's Day suddenly felt like a nagging reminder of all the things I didn't have or hadn't achieved the year before.

Thoughts bombarded my mind such as, *You always choose the wrong path, Kristin. If you had just made better choices, you would have what you desire by now.* By this point in my life, I was *certain* I would have a stable career, a happy marriage, three or four kids, a nice house. Instead, life hadn't turned out the way I'd imagined it would. I was job-less, marriage-less, and child-less, while experiencing delay after delay toward my goals. It didn't make sense—especially since I'm a goal-oriented person.

Instead of checking my list of goals off as accomplished, it seemed like my dreams had been dashed like a game of Rock-Paper-Scissors. I felt as I was hearing, *Sorry Kristin, paper covers rock…you lose again!* Consequently, instead of trusting my life path to God, I became preoccupied with proving. Proving hard to myself and others that I was "adulting" well. I thought having certain assets would make me valuable.

I felt a need to attain something, *anything* that would make me equal to the people I admired, who had already accomplished certain material milestones by now. Shame had reliably reared its ugly head once again as I lamented over the previous year's setbacks. Have you ever thought, *Why am I not further along in life by now? Why does it seem like I've barely moved an inch in twelve months?*

There are two kinds of losses in life: things you've *had* that were taken away, and dreams you *want* that haven't come to pass. When it's hard for me to trust God's plans are good, even with the setbacks I've experienced, I return to certain scriptures to strengthen my heart. If it's challenging for you to trust God's plan in the midst of your heartbreaks, try reflecting on this scripture, which emphasizes God's promise that He will bring restoration (healing) to you. "I will restore to you the years that the swarming locust has eaten" Joel 2:25.

This scripture is a promise from God that He will bring restoration. Restoration of the energy, joy, and peace that life's heartbreaks have stolen from you. After repeated detours, delays, and dead ends, you can feel depleted. Deep disappointment can rob you of the sweet innocence you had as a child, when your heart was filled with confidence, hope, and the promises of good things to come. After prolonged seasons of pain, you can forget what that kind of joy feels like. It's hard to remember the last time you felt happy, peaceful, or hopeful about life. The promise from God in the book of Joel assures us that we *can* and *will* experience peace and joy again one day, whether on this earth or in eternity when we will be with Him forever. God says *He will restore your years of pain and heartache.* Isn't that hopeful news?

HeartBRAKE #9

When I first decided to follow Christ, all I had to do was read the promises of God, like the one found in the book of Joel, and I instantly believed them. I was so filled with hope early on in my journey that believing wasn't difficult. However, after multiple seasons of setbacks and delays, it's not as easy to read a verse or a passage of scripture and automatically believe what it says. If I'm being honest, I've struggled to believe God's Word at times. I *wanted* to put my trust in what it said, but I had a difficult time finding the faith to believe it. Yet, through persevering through hard times, I've learned that it's only by *meditating* on the Word, not just reading it, that I find hope again. God's Word declares, "Faith comes by hearing, and hearing by the word of God" (Romans 10:17). When I hear God's Word, meditate on it, and envision Him interacting with me intimately, my faith begins to grow.

One of my favorite promises from God is found in the Book of Isaiah:

> Those who wait on the Lord shall renew their strength; they shall mount up with wings like eagles, they shall run and not be weary, they shall walk and not faint (Isaiah 40:31).

In other words, when you wait upon God (meditate upon His Word, linger in it, park on the same verse, read the passage over and over again) and pause on His promises (eagerly desiring, anticipating, longing for them), your strength and hope will return. Waiting upon God turned out to be a restorative experience. As I saturated my mind with Isaiah 40, I sensed the Holy Spirit saying, *The path to freedom is paved with detours, delays, and times of dryness.* Those words rang in my ears. I thought about them until I finally realized, *If we didn't ever experience being stagnant or stuck, how would we ever truly appreciate freedom from setbacks and shame?*

Have you experienced holiday heartbreak shame? Have repeated relationship delays left you feeling disappointed? Does your heart long to be free from the pain of shame caused by another delay? Could it be that God is strengthening His relationship with you through this arduous path?

Mature, heart-healing love is born through the freedom acquired *after* enduring recurring delays. I'm not talking about the DIY, manufactured, kind of freedom. I'm talking about what the woman at the well experienced. The kind of freedom found only in God's presence.

Life Lesson

Jesus's living water quenches your thirst and sets you free from shame so you can become all you are meant to be. His freedom is a lasting kind of freedom that make you better. Stronger. More like Christ. God will heal and strengthen you through each and every holiday heartbreak, as you spend time drinking in the water of His beautiful, irresistible presence.

HeartBRAKE #9

Shame-Stopping Scripture: "Not that I speak in regard to need, for I have learned in whatever state I am, to be content" (Philippians 4:11). What situation do you need to practice contentment in? How might God be inviting you to experience His presence and fill you with His living water?

____

____

____

____

____

HeartBRAKE #10
The Shame of Seduction

Let me paint another picture for you as I talk about a very prevalent kind of heartbreak shame—the shame of seduction. Has your car ever been stuck in the mud or snow? It's a frustrating experience, to say the least. Imagine this scenario, and as you recall this instant replay, let's suppose your heart is this car. It's stuck in the muddy, icy, sleet of disappointment, and the wheels are spinning frantically in place, trying to get out of it. Does this sound familiar?

You're driving along the highway of life when suddenly you realize your tires are wedged into place. You try to move forward… to no avail. You begin to sweat. You rehearse negative outcomes. You get a pit in your stomach, right before you gun the engine. Yet the harder you press on the pedal, the more your wheels spin, desperately trying to gain traction. You yell at the car, "GO!" secretly hoping your words will somehow propel your vehicle forward. Unfortunately, after all your effort, your tires are even more jammed in place.

In a last-ditch attempt to get free, you press on the gas once again, hoping that by putting the pedal to the metal, you will gain momentum.

This effort only exacerbates the problem. Now your wheels are spinning even faster. Smoke is pouring out of the exhaust pipe, and you're going nowhere. You can't move in either direction. *You're officially stuck in place!*

Has your heart felt like an immobilized car, lodged into a fixed position? You've been dealt many disappointing blows, and now you're paralyzed by shame. You can't move. You've revved up the engine of your heart time after time. You try to move forward once more toward your dreams and goals, but no traction is gained. You are stuck yet again in an unwanted, heartbreaking place.

Like an engine in danger of overheating, our hearts are vulnerable to temptation when we're disappointed. Like an incapacitated car looking for a way out, we want to gun the accelerator and fast track our way past the pain. We tell ourselves that speeding through the pain will help us reach our destination more quickly and provide relief from the shame of unfulfilled desires. This attempt to speed through disappointment is one time when temptation entices us to take a ride.

We have our weakest moments when we feel discouraged. Think back to a situation when you were tempted to do something you knew was wrong. What, or who, enticed you? Perhaps this situation or person came along when you were more vulnerable than ever. You've been in the same place for years without change. You're in an unsatisfying career, a difficult relationship, or super stressful time in your life.

What haven't you been able to make happen in your life, even though you've tried? You don't *want* to compromise your values or integrity to make gains, but at this point you are seriously *tempted* to. You want results, and you want them now. Suddenly, an attractive option comes along. You consider revving the engine of your heart and taking a shortcut toward your dreams. But you know temptation is a slippery slope; you could lose control of your car completely if you go over the speed limit. So you stay put for a while, flirting with the fantasy of what you *could* do.

As you sit tight in park, white-knuckling the gear shift, tempting thoughts swirl through your mind. *The battle has begun.* You're fully aware that if you take this path, there's no telling where it will lead. Part of you doesn't care. You're curious. More than ever, you want to know what it feels like to travel at high speeds with the wind whipping through your hair. *In the blink of an eye, you move into fifth gear.*

Can you recall a time when you decided to move into the fast lane of life? A time when things weren't working out according to your plans? A time you wanted to take a shorter route because the journey was taking too long to hold on? A time when you put the pedal to the metal to power past the disillusionment? Instead of listening to your navigator (a.k.a. the Holy Spirit) you speed up, hoping to reach your destination faster.

What could cause you to shift into overdrive so rapidly? In this case, it is seduction. Fantasy provides the fuel for your engine's fire, and the thrill of a risky ride revs your heart up. Suddenly you're catapulted forward, swiftly gaining speed. Temptation's lustful lure has made you an offer, and you willfully accept. *The wild ride has now begun.*

One tempestuous time, during a particularly dry season in my life, the wheels of my heart lost traction, wedged under the weight of unfulfilled desires. I felt defenseless against the despair hovering over me. My dreams felt like the fumes of a dried-up engine, gasping for fuel and oil. My growing disconnection from the Holy Spirit was palpable. I tried to stay put as I contemplated two paths: the path of self-will, or the path of alignment with God's purpose for me. I knew I had a choice. I could reconnect with the Holy Spirit and ask Him to give me the strength to trust Him. Or I could accelerate on my own and see where it would take me. I knew discouragement had made its home in my heart. I was weary from the trail of dead-end dreams. I was tired of all the tangled up, tear-stained trials. Willfully, I gave in to the temptation to take a shortcut. Impulsively, I drove to dangerously high speeds, losing control of my heart during the ride.

It happened after a long season of career and relationship drought. Hoping it would energize me to live life with passion again, I started a new job. That's when I met Stan. He had a captivating personality and strong leadership skills. Over time, we began to share our ideas with one another about how to implement effective strategies within the organization and in our community. I had no intention of being anything more than a friend to Stan, especially since he and I were coworkers.

One night when I was working late at the office, I received a call with an unusual twist. It was Stan, and it began as a harmless chat. We started laughing and sharing ideas as usual. Then something changed. Stan began speaking in a different tone of voice. He told me he needed someone to talk to, someone who would understand his dilemma. *What dilemma*, I wondered. Stan went on to say he and his wife were having marital problems. He asked for my advice about his situation, as he complimented me about how easy it was to talk to me, and how compassionate I was.

Suddenly I found myself pumping the brakes. Now that I knew Stan was married, I was even more adamant about keeping our relationship professional. I knew it was unwise for me to engage in conversations with him that would put us both in a vulnerable place. That's what my *head* said. However, my *heart* said something completely different. My heart was drawn to him, drawn to the conversations and compliments.

It's ok to talk to Stan, I told myself. *You're not doing anything wrong. You can be friends, just guard your heart.* I thought if I kept reminding myself to guard my heart, I would be okay. I didn't realize that my initial attempt at setting boundaries would be no match for Satan's subtle snare. After that pivotal conversation when Stan opened up his heart to me, things began to speed up instead of slow down. My car was shifting into overdrive, and I knew it. I yielded to the temptation of acceleration, to get relief from the complacency I felt in my life. I put myself in places where I knew Stan would be. I looked forward to the late-night conversations, where more personal information was shared between us.

I started developing feelings for Stan. A war was going on between my mind and my heart. The logical part of me kept calculating how to have the right balance of connection with an equal amount of space. My heart, however, increasingly desired to spend more and more time with him. No matter how hard I tried to regulate the route, fantasies of Stan gained control of the wheel, as they seductively steered my heart in his direction.

A simple definition of temptation is, "The desire to do something that is unwise or wrong."[8] Do you know you have a loving Heavenly Father who doesn't want you to make unwise choices outside of His purposes for you? He wants to protect you from the pain seduction brings. We see this temptation play out in the book of Genesis. Adam and Eve experienced temptation when they decided to do something God told them not to. Yet Satan made the situation appear so desirable, they gave in. God knew the heartbreaks they would endure and the shame that would follow if they didn't heed His warning. However, He allowed them to have free will, just like He has given to us (Genesis 3:1-6).

The temptation I was experiencing was an intimate relationship with a married man who I was very attracted to. I knew deep down this relationship wasn't God's will for me. Yet just like Eve, I began wanting what I shouldn't want. Desiring what I shouldn't desire. Instead of resisting and running from temptation, I drove right toward it. Second Timothy 2:22 advises us to "Flee lust." What is lust? It is unrestrained passion. I knew I was lusting in my heart, but I didn't want to flee from it. Instead, like a NASCAR driver, I sped right past the boundaries I'd previously put in place. Before long, I was going ninety miles per hour in a twenty-five mile per hour zone, heading straight for a collision.

The Holy Spirit, in His lovingkindness, provided some speed bumps along the way. Then one merciful day, when I hit one of them, I finally made the choice to slow down. Don't get me wrong, I had a hard time taking this step. My feelings for Stan had deepened, and I didn't want to stop interacting with him. Nevertheless, I decided to call my boss and tell him about the situation. He thanked me for sharing my dilemma with him, and very compassionately, yet firmly, told me what I needed to do to remain true to my convictions. His advice included putting a practical plan in place to stop things from escalating.

Have you been in a situation when you knew the right thing to do, but your heart longed to give into the lust you craved anyway? I know firsthand how easy it is to ignore the guidance of others when you want to yield to temptation. Even though I had the support of my boss, I knew it was going to take *God's* strength to overcome this battle. After getting a game plan in place, I initiated a conversation with Stan to introduce my idea to him. I told him it wasn't good for us to have heart-to-hearts and rendezvous for two. We discussed all the parameters we needed to put in place. Since we were colleagues, I knew it wouldn't be easy. I even thought about quitting. However, I told myself that wasn't necessary, and remained hopeful that Stan would respect my plans to remain in park, rather than overdrive.

Unfortunately, after our nice little convo, our engines didn't cool. They only got hotter.

In no time, Stan started pushing past my parameters, and I could feel my heart revving up again—this time, even more than before—and I didn't want to slow down. I was being seduced. I felt weaker than ever, yet I convinced myself I could handle it. The Apostle Paul says, "Let him who thinks he stands take heed lest he fall" (1 Corinthians 10:12 NKJV). *In other words, don't tell yourself you can handle temptation on your own.* If the Holy Spirit and other people are not invited to help you out, you *will* fall into sin. The more I tried to control the situation in my own strength, the more manipulative Stan became. I thought I was gaining strength and spiritual authority, but instead I was losing it. The deception was subtle at first, yet unmistakably real. I deceived myself into believing I had the upper hand. I thought I had regained control of the wheel, but the car was quickly veering off into the fast lane.

One morning, I was in the office working on a project when Stan approached me.

"Kristin," he said, "can I talk to you for a minute?"

My heart pounded. Before I knew it, I was practically at his feet. "Yes, Stan, what is it?" I whispered, trying to remain composed.

"Would you meet me at the Courtyard Inn tonight?" he asked, matter-of-factly. "We don't have to tell anyone."

I froze inside. *Stan just asked me to meet him at a hotel.* I will never forget how I felt in that moment. There I stood, six inches from Stan's face, knowing if he tried to kiss me I wouldn't say no. Fumbling over my words, I replied, "No, Stan, I can't meet you." Then I looked for the nearest exit, and I left the building. I drove home feeling extremely weak from the weight of temptation; my flesh desperately wanted to give in to Stan's request. Fighting to stay abstinent until marriage hadn't seemed to pay off. I thought about all the time (the days, weeks, months, and years) I had spent surrendering my sexual desires to God and choosing celibacy, after passionately pursuing empty, meaningless sex early on in my dating life. I knew God's desire is for single believers to abstain from sex until marriage. Yet it seemed like this decision hadn't paid off the way I'd expected it to. I couldn't understand why this winding road of detours, delays, and dead ends was my path. How long would I have to keep living this way? I knew in the depths of my heart that sexual pleasure, apart from God's will, wasn't worth it. Does God love us when we fall short of His will? Absolutely! There's nothing we could ever, *ever* do to separate ourselves from His abounding love. Yet his Spirit was restraining me. On a gut level, I knew that getting entangled with a married man would only lead to heartbreak shame and worse pain down the road.

That afternoon, I prayed a silent prayer of lament to God asking for strength, *Lord, lead me not into temptation, but deliver me from evil* (Matthew 6:13). Then I closed my eyes. Sometimes God has an interesting way of answering our prayers. It doesn't always happen the way we expect. This time, God answered my prayer through a dream. I dreamt I was with Stan. He whispered something incoherent in my ear right before he kissed it. Then, as soon as I let him kiss me, Stan turned into a snake and bit me. When I woke up, I instantly had clarity. Satan was trying to lead me down a path of temptation so I would be seduced into compromising my most heartfelt convictions. God had a purpose for me to fulfill and *this* wasn't part of it. Just like Satan (the serpent) tempted Eve in the garden, he was cunningly trying to seduce me away from God's destiny for my life.

With every ounce of strength I had, I called a close friend of mine and asked her to pray for me. I told her I needed God to get me out of a situation I was in. She prayed, "Lord, I don't know how You're going to do it, but I am asking You to fight for my friend." A few days later, Stan left the job without any explanation. He wrote a letter to our employer, simply saying he would not be returning, and then he quit. I was so grateful that the Lord protected me from what I know would have escalated into a physical affair with a married man. Stan tried to contact me a few months later. He told me that he and his wife were divorcing, and he hoped we could meet and talk. "No thank you," I said emphatically.

In Stan's absence, God had given me the strength I needed to "detox" him from my heart, as well as giving me the insight I needed to move on. Stan wasn't worth compromising my relationship with God or my conviction to marry a man with integrity. Stan did not fit that description.

In many ways, the situation with Stan was heartbreaking. It was heartbreaking to fall for a married man. It was heartbreaking to grieve another relationship loss. However, looking back, I see how God kept me from even *more* pain— the shame I would've experienced if I'd had an affair with a married man, and the aftermath that would have ensued.

Maybe someone reading my story is being seduced right now. Maybe you are experiencing temptation at this very moment or you're already involved sexually with a married man or woman. Please know I am *not* condemning you. I truly empathize with your pain. I have walked in your shoes of weakness, vulnerability, and longing. It's difficult to fight against the flesh. It's especially heartbreaking to fall in love with someone who is committed to someone else. It's also heartbreaking to be betrayed, if you're the one who was cheated on. With the rise of social media, chat apps, dating sites, and people you can connect with at the touch of a button, or swipe of the wrist, the temptation to engage in fantasy, pornography, or real-life sexual escapades as a way of life, is increasing. We live in a culture of seduction, and having sex-on-demand has almost been normalized as a human "right."

Yet, that's not God's best for you. God can and will strengthen you in the midst of temptation. He will provide a way out of any sexual entanglement and enticement if you ask Him too. He will even give you the grace to end an affair, if you're in one. He can also heal you from any heartbreak shame that comes from the pain of sexual seduction. Jesus loves to restore broken hearts and free you from shame.

Thankfully the shame of seduction didn't linger long with Stan.

However, the year I turned forty was another story. That year I attempted to take another shortcut to circumvent God's provision for me. The gear in my heart suddenly shifted again when the reality of becoming older, combined with unfulfilled desires, resurfaced. I was tired of holding onto my convictions without seeing tangible results. Instead, right in front of me, was a golden opportunity for love and romance with a man I met at the gym. Before long, temptation took the wheel. This time, at a very vulnerable point in the journey, I chose to get out of *my* car and into the car of a man named Keith, who did not believe in, or follow after God at all. That's when the temptation to comprise my values really ramped up.

I knew I wanted to marry someone who shared the same faith as me, which clearly, Keith did not. I knew the Word of God advised against this for good reasons. For example, The Apostle Paul instructs believers in Christ not to be "unequally yoked together with unbelievers" (2 Corinthians 6:14 NASB). In this context, a yoke is a device used to tie oxen together for farming purposes. If both oxen are weighted correctly, they will pull each other in the same direction for maximum production and the most beneficial agricultural results. If two oxen are improperly yoked or carrying different weights, they will attempt to go in the same direction, but will eventually succumb to pulling each other in circles, accomplishing nothing.

The Bible equates this simple farming example with our choice of a mate. When you are unequally yoked, it means one person loves and follows God and the other person doesn't. When that happens, the same outcome applies. Two people going in different directions cannot successfully help each other grow in their faith. A good example to read for practical understanding is the story of Samson and Delilah in Judges 16. Here we witness Samson falling in love with a woman (Delilah) who does not love, worship, or acknowledge the God Samson loves. As the story unfolds, Samson gradually gives his heart to her. The union eventually goes south when Delilah's impure motives win out over Samson's godly mission. If you are considering dating or marrying someone who does not share your Christ-like values, I encourage you to read this story and pray for insight.

I knew the risks of dating Keith, yet I was tired of waiting for Mr. Right, and Keith was a very attractive alternative. Right from the start it felt good being next to him, as he flirted with me while drinking his Frappuccino. I loved accepting affection from a man who knew how to steal a girl's heart. He took me out on the town and treated me to the finer things in life. Being with him suddenly seemed so appealing. Tempting thoughts began swirling in my mind, "Why stay in my own broken-down dumpster of a ride going nowhere, when I could catch a ride with someone who seems to have it all, instead? Someone who could lead me out of the land of loneliness, toward the isle of desire. Oh, the dreamy, creamy, thrill of temptation. It feels so good in the beginning. It's like eating dark chocolate; sweet at first, with a bitter bite mixed into the succulent blend.

Have you been tempted to disconnect from the core of who you are and everything you believe in, to slip into someone else's nice, sleek, ride instead? In the movie *Addicted,* the character Marcella reveals a married woman's battle as she goes down the path of temptation, right into the trap of sexual addiction. In the beginning, Marcella attempts to meet her unfulfilled longings by watching pornography and fantasizing about being with other men. Then she engages in a seemingly harmless flirtation with a man she meets in person, which escalates until they are in bed together. Her behavior quickly spirals out of control, becoming more and more risky and seductive. As she yields unrelentingly to her desires, she starts having not just one, but two affairs. Before long, she is so entangled in lust that she is in danger of losing her job, her family, and everything that is near and dear to her. Lust is an insidious snare. It will lure you right into a den of darkness, stripping you of all self-control and self-worth, and clothing you in shame instead.

Sexual fantasies, racy photos, seductive conversations, erotic videos, and illicit affairs are attempts to meet unfulfilled emotional needs. Sometimes, turning to these things is an effort to cover up how you really feel about yourself, or to mask unresolved pain from the past. Other times, it's a way to cope with undesirable feelings such as being alone, or with unwanted circumstances like feeling dissatisfied in a relationship. Marcella's cravings went from an unmet emotional need to a physical and psychological addiction. We are *all* vulnerable to temptation, and it's easy to be enticed by lust in today's culture. "Sexual addiction is a phenomenon we're hearing more and more about these days."[9] In my experience as a clinician, it appears that sexually addictive and compulsive behaviors are on the rise, for men *and* women. The problem with sexual lust is that it's insatiable. The more you get what you crave, the more you want it. It's a deep, shame-filled, bottomless pit.

Maybe you're being tempted right now. If you are, you would be no different than most people in this world. In fact, you would be just like Jesus Himself. The Bible says that Jesus was in all ways tempted like we are, yet without sin (Hebrews 4:15). Lust is a common temptation and a difficult battle to overcome. So how did Jesus fight against it? *Only with God's help*, with the escape route(s) The Holy Spirit continually provided for Him. God tells us we *are* able overcome lust with His strength. Temptation is common to man, "but God is faithful, who will not allow you to be tempted beyond what you are able, but with the temptation will also make the way of escape" (1 Corinthians 10:13). God provides us with an exit route, *if we'll take it.*

This is exactly what God did when I was tempted in my relationship with Keith. The more time I spent with him, the more I knew Keith wasn't right for me. In fact, I felt exactly like Samson being seduced by Delilah. Yet God proved to be faithful to His Word. When things began to spiral out of control, Jesus provided a way of escape. I tried to protect my heart, but my efforts crumbled as I became addicted to the excitement of Keith's flattery and company. Chemicals (such as oxytocin) fired rapidly in my brain, bonding us together. I was like a teenager experiencing her first crush. One night after a fun date with Keith, I initiated a kiss that lit my entire being on fire and overtook my mind with thoughts of lust and desire. *There is no escape*, I thought. *It's too late.* My flesh and spirit were warring against each other, and my flesh was winning. Nevertheless, as hard as it was to put an end to the passion, I said good night, went in the house and closed the door on desire. Yet thoughts of Keith swirled in my mind all night long.

Just when I thought there was no turning back from the perilous path of passion I'd chosen, the very next day I heard a knock on my door. I opened it to find a friend of mine, Nate, looking at me with compassion and holding three white lilies in his hands. "I don't know why, but I felt like I just had to come here," Nate said as he handed me the lilies. "I can't explain it. I'm not sure what you're going through right now, but I was compelled to come to your house and remind you of God's love for you." Before he even finished speaking, I burst into tears.

White lilies had always been special to me, and I knew God sent Nate to remind me of the covenant I made with Christ years ago when I decided to give my heart to Him. I was overwhelmed with emotion because that's when I realized *Nate's visit was my way of escape.* It was as if God Himself had shown up at my door. Knocking on my heart. Showering me with His love, right in the middle of my temptation to turn away from Him.

God created a protective barrier between me and Keith with His love. He reminded me that *Jesus* is "the one" who will give me everything I need, just like He reminded Gomer in the book of Hosea. When Gomer pursued other lovers, God hedged up the way with thorns, and persuaded her that *He* was who she really wanted. He was the one who would supply her every need (Hosea 2:5-8). God was providing a way of escape for me *with His passionate pursuit of my heart.* All I had to do was take it.

So I did.

That's not to say it was easy. In fact, it was very difficult. The emotional turmoil my soul went through as I detached from Keith was difficult at times. It isn't easy to trust God's plan, even when you know how much He loves you and feel His heart wooing you back toward Him. I still had to go through a grieving process as I was letting go of what my soul longed for and had become so attached to. Just as God provides escape routes out of the grip of seduction, He also provides opportunities for healing, such as counseling, after you've succumbed to temptation and been swallowed up by shame. Sometimes we don't *want* a way of escape and choose to enter situations we know aren't good for us. We rationalize, justify, compromise, and do things in our own self-will.

But God has "lilies" for you too.

Whether God speaks to you through flesh flowers or something else, He will reveal His abundant faithfulness.

He wants to show up in your life and bring you the love you deserve. He wants to shower you with His kindness in the midst of your longing, in the midst of your darkest night and hardest battle. He is *always* fighting for you!

When has seduction led you down a heartbreaking path? Perhaps it's happening right now. (Genesis 3:1-6). Satan knows exactly how to tempt you. He did it with Jesus. "After Jesus had fasted forty days and forty nights, he was hungry" (Matthew 4:2). Satan knew what Jesus would be hungry for, so he tempted him with his desires. "If thou be the Son of God, command these stones to be made into bread" (Matthew 4:3).

What desires do you have? Is it a desire to be loved? To be accepted? Is it a desire for something or someone you've wanted for a very long time? Maybe it's a desire to take a shortcut around the path God has for you. Human desires are not wrong. It's only when the desire turns into an idol and throws you off track from your purpose in God that it turns into heartbreak shame.

Giving into seduction leads to heartbreak because lust is not love. When you go against your conscience and allow lust to lead the way, when you cheat on your partner, or replace authentic intimacy with porn, it will only be followed by shame. In addition to being seduced by sex, you can also be seduced to doubt God's plan and take a shortcut around the path He has predestined for your life. You can be seduced to live according to other people's expectations of you, or to hold on to something God wants you to let go of.

I have endured many temptations along the way. Temptation is part of the journey of life. The Bible says we should expect it. "Do not think it strange concerning the fiery trial which is to try you, as though some strange thing happened to you" (1 Peter 4:12). If you are being tested and tempted, it's not strange at all. It's normal.

Whenever you face a temptation, God will give you a restless feeling inside if it is something He doesn't want you to do. That's the conviction of the Holy Spirit. It takes determination to surrender to God's will as you wrestle through the battle of temptation. Determination increases through prayer, reading God's Word, and talking with other temptation-fighters who can help you navigate challenging situations.

Life Lesson

Be encouraged—God always provides exit routes away from seduction, and when you take them you will be rewarded. He can and will heal any heartbreak shame that seduction has seared upon your soul.

HeartBRAKE #10

Shame-Stopping Scripture: "No temptation has overtaken you except such as is common to man; but God is faithful, who will not allow you to be tempted beyond what you are able, but with the temptation will also make the way of escape, that you may be able to bear it" (1 Corinthians 10:13).Where are you being tempted right now? Do you need a way of escape out of the snare of seduction? If you pray, God will provide you with one!

____

____

____

____

____

____

HeartBRAKE #11
The Shame of Addiction

Every heartbreak can leave an imprint of shame on your soul, yet one kind of heartbreak that is particularly shameful is the heartbreak of addiction. There is nothing quite as cunning, baffling, or powerful as the grip of addiction on someone's life. Today's world is filled with opportunities for all kinds of substance abuse, and in the wake of Covid-19, addiction is on the rise. Yet unlike the virus, there is no vaccine for addiction. Just as we are experiencing an international health pandemic, addiction is a pandemic of its own kind, on a similar global scale.

The United States opioid crisis is leading the charge in overdoses, sucking the life out of those who are trapped in its demonic grip and devastating the lives of those who love them. Fentanyl addiction is also climbing and killing those left in its wake. This insidious substance is now found in heroin and other drugs such as crack and methamphetamines making them even more dangerous. Alcohol abuse isn't far behind opioid addiction, and because it's culturally acceptable and woven into the fabric of many events, it can be challenging to identify as problematic, even for alcoholics themselves. Many people who are dealing with anxiety and stress are relying on Benzodiazepines, highly potent anti-anxiety drugs, to calm their brains. Although pills like Xanax and Valium are closely regulated by the FDA, they are very addictive, and they are being abused.

And that's not all people are addicted to these days. With technology literally at the tips of our fingers, more and more people are addicted to pornography, online sex, gaming, gambling, social media, Netflix, and their phones in general. As a society, we can't stay off our phones. We are texting people in the same house from different rooms. Face to face contact is diminishing and being replaced with videos, texts, and social media chats. One client of mine regretfully shared feeling like she'd lost *years* of her life to a YouTube addiction. A lack of intimacy and connection with others was the precursor to evenings spent glued to YouTube—yet a lack of intimacy and connection with others was *also* the result. Can you relate? What is monopolizing your time more than you want it to? What's filling you up when you feel lonely or disconnected?

Over the course of my life, I've experienced the pain of addiction and the subsequent heartbreak shame which follows. Only during the past couple of years have I even been able to *say* the word addiction as it pertains to my own experience and *admit* it's been a problem for me. *After all, who likes the word addiction? Or likes to say they're an addict?* My guess is, the vast majority do not.

I certainly didn't.

I preferred to say I had an unhealthy relationship with alcohol and needed to cut back. Or that I was using substances to "cope" but I certainly wasn't *addicted.* Not me. I had my own business, place to live, car, and rich relationships with others. It wasn't until I was brought to my knees in humility that I could join the ranks of the warriors *willing to admit* they are dependent on a substance which steals their sanity and serenity. For me, it was alcohol and benzodiazepines. Namely, wine and Xanax. It was a long journey towards admitting it was a problem, seeking help, and getting into recovery, of which I am still a part. I want to share my dark spiral downward, in hopes that perhaps my story will play a small part in bringing healing to *your* story.

Alcohol always seemed to be a part of my life, at least as far back as early adolescence when I first experimented with friends. Looking back, even the experimental stage didn't quite seem normal. I vaguely recall drinking too much right from the start. I don't even remember if I liked it or not. But I do remember trying to make mixed drinks that were heavy on the liquor and light on the mixer, which didn't go over so well with my teenage body. Even more memorable was the fact that alcohol was always paired with relationship bonding. Even at a young age, I bonded with friends while using liquor to do it. We had crazy fun in the moment, and lots of risky adventures. It was the after-affect I didn't like so much. The weekend binges and benders, the muted memories, poor decisions, close calls in cars, late night fights, and next day regrets. As the years went on, I thought I could manage my intake better and drink moderately, like other people did. Sometimes I could and sometimes I couldn't. It was a game of Russian Roulette, so to speak.

At one point, I decided to stop playing that game and quit drinking altogether for ten years, only rarely having a glass of wine during that time. Then my drinking picked back up in the Bible belt, of all places. It was fellow Christians who told me that, according to the Bible, I could drink in moderation, as long as I was intentional about "moderating." *Hmm, maybe I'll give this another try,* I thought. For several years, it worked out okay. I'm not exactly sure when it flipped, or what made it flip. But nevertheless, it *did* indeed flip. Somehow, somewhere along the way, I stopped being able to control my drinking. And thus, the path toward addiction took a sharp left turn.

I could blame the problem on many things if I wanted to: *age, hormones, disappointments, increased anxiety, job stress, life stress, and still being single though my heart longed for marriage.* These things "drove me to drink" I thought and gave me a reason to relax and escape from the cares of life for a bit. If my "moderating" wasn't a problem, however, then why was I so often filled with guilt and inner turmoil about it? *Maybe I'm being too religious,* I thought. *After all, a lot of people drink regularly. It's okay to enjoy life. Even Jesus turned water into wine.* These are the things I told myself when I felt bad about my drinking; usually the next day after I'd said I would only drink two, but had five instead.

Then there was the shame. *Where did that come from?* I looked at the diagnostic criteria for alcoholism to see if I fit the bill, but I never quite did. Alcohol wasn't destroying my life or my relationships. I still held a job and had friends. I didn't have any DUIs, I hadn't gone to jail or wrecked anything. Yet something wasn't right, and deep down I knew it. Alcohol seemed to be on my mind a whole lot. I was preoccupied with it. If I wasn't drinking, it was because I planned not to drink or I was giving myself a break from it. When I was drinking, I was pacing myself or trying to control it by planning how many to have or not have that day. It was like an obsession of sorts. *Do normal drinkers think this way?* I wondered. I could never find the answers I so desperately sought. And then there was the fact that alcohol seemed to be a part of almost every occasion, so the same question was always on the table: *Will I drink at this event or not?* This question seemed to always be on my mind in one way or another.

Then life took some unfortunate turns. More heartbreak shame came—the end of a relationship and the closing of my church and my business. I scrambled to find a job to get my head above water again. It was all starting to weigh heavily on me. Too many disappointments in life. Wrong turns. Regrets. Fears about the future. Drinking seemed to ease the pain a bit. Especially wine. Boy did I love that! Give me a Sauvignon blanc or a rosé, and life suddenly seemed grand again. For the moment anyway.

Yet all of that changed unexpectedly somehow. Over time I began to *need* to drink, not just want to. And if I drank too much? Well, I had Xanax for that. To help me sleep and deal with the shame I felt before bed, or when I woke up the next morning. I kept talking myself out of having a problem, though, because "so and so drinks more than me" or "I'm not an alcoholic because I could stop if I really wanted to." So I did. I took breaks. I cut back. I stopped for a few weeks, or months at a time. Yet every time I picked up a drink again, it was more than just a drink: it was a camaraderie, a companionship, a relief from emotional pain.

And then there were those peculiar behaviors, including the nights I would hide my drinking or sneak a drink when others weren't around. Who was I hiding it from? I was an adult. Why was I having a drink before the party then another one after it, all by myself? *Just because I'm not telling anyone doesn't mean I'm doing something wrong…does it?* Maybe it felt like a secret because I knew in my heart it *was* a secret. Yet even though I knew something wasn't right I pushed my concerns far, far away so I could continue to "enjoy" what I now loved most in life—*alcohol.*

I once heard someone say there's no such thing as "rock bottom" because as long as you're still alive the bottom can always go lower. Something about that seems true. Nevertheless, my drinking did have a bottom. At least one low enough to bring me to my knees, as I cried out for help. It was during a night alone, filled with emotions I couldn't quite name and a fridge full of wine calling my name. If only it had stopped there, drinking a few too many at home alone, but it didn't. Suddenly I got a call from a friend and I was off to the races. The next thing I knew I was at a bar. *How did I get here?* I think I drove.

Why am I drinking more?

I certainly didn't need to. The train of logical reasoning had jumped the track, and I was turning into someone I didn't recognize or want to be.

That night turned into a complete blur. Parts of it I remember and parts I don't. Several bars later and then someone else's apartment. Rides around town from people I didn't know. A guy from my work crashing at my house. All I know is I woke up the next morning thinking I had lost my mind. My nerves were so bad I was popping Xanax as I drank my coffee. "God," I prayed, "please don't let me go crazy." The next thing I know I'm packing my bags, and then I went to stay with a friend, convincing myself I just need some time away.

I really wanted to check myself into the hospital for a few days. Find some relief from the pain. I couldn't escape the four horsemen—terror, bewilderment, frustration, and despair. That time was just one of many episodes where I simply couldn't stop drinking and taking pills to relieve pain. When did normal, moderate drinking turn into behind the wheel, at a random bar, saying-and-doing-things-I-will-regret-later drinking. *What was happening to me?*

One night, after a few weeks of abstaining, I couldn't wait to drink again: first wine, then specialty drinks at a festive holiday party. I convinced myself I could drive home, since I was only a few miles away, but my head was in such a fog I turned on my phone navigator for extra guidance. Before I knew it, my phone died and I was in the middle of nowhere. *How did I get here? How will I get home?* Fear enveloped me like a heavy storm cloud full of rain. There I was—lost at a gas station, with a dead phone, in the middle of nowhere.

I swear it was an angel who helped me get home. This woman appeared out of the blue and told me to follow her down the highway and she would lead me to wherever I needed to go. If my bed was in Heaven, I would have kissed God's feet that night as I cried and thanked Him for not letting me or anyone else die on my way home. The next day I was so scared of my behavior the night before that I finally tried to check myself into a hospital and tell the doctor I thought I had bipolar disorder. "I'm having a manic episode," I said emphatically. The doctor just smiled and said, "You're not manic, but too much alcohol can make you think you are. You should check out some programs in the area if you need some help." I thought to myself, *Well if I'm an alcoholic, and if alcoholics have rock bottoms, I definitely hit one last night.* And if alcoholics have "tops," I found one in recovery. What I mean is that although I dared not admit I was an alcoholic at first, once I did, boy-oh-boy it felt great to finally face *reality* and find *freedom* from my obsession with alcohol—

one day at a time. When I joined a group and went to meetings with other people who struggled with drinking like me, I was empowered to begin recovering from the grip alcohol had on me. It was a relief to hear similar stories and others' battles with substance abuse. Some stories I could relate to and others I couldn't, but one thing we all had in common was an unhealthy obsession with alcohol and a desire to change.

As I continued down the journey of recovery and daily surrender of the obsession to drink, there was one thing I knew for sure. Our minds are a battlefield, and we need to yield to God's plan if we want to fulfill our destiny. When you have a destiny, strongholds like addiction love to chokehold the life out of it. Satan will gladly steal, kill, and destroy *any* plans you have that are purposeful for the Kingdom of God. You just need to have the right armor on so you can fight back. God's Word encourages us to "Be sober, be diligent because Satan is as a roaring lion seeking whom he may devour" (1 Peter 5:8). The devil relentlessly devours addicts and their loved ones whenever and wherever he can. I experienced the truth of that verse when one of my ex-boyfriends passed away years ago from an opioid and alcohol addiction. That's when the destruction of the disease really hit home for me. The reality that young people *can* and *do* die daily was not just a statistic anymore. It was now a part of my life. Addiction does not discriminate. *Yet freedom through Christ is freely available to anyone who seeks it.* I know this firsthand, as someone who has fought ferociously for this freedom and found it to be true.

It took many meetings, medication trials, and detoxing my system before my brain chemistry started to feel normal again—and if I'm being honest, it's still a battle—but knowing God is always fighting on my behalf keeps me strong!

Maybe you don't have a chemical addiction, but you're in a relationship with someone who does. There can be much shame in that journey too. It is painful to love an addict and to ride the roller coaster of addiction with them. You may feel like no one understands. Or you might be afraid that others will judge your journey. The more you hide it from others, the more shame you feel. It can be difficult to decide how much support to offer someone who is battling addiction and when to draw boundaries or walk away.

Counseling can be extremely helpful in this process. Secrecy is part of the cycle of addiction, but there is healing in talking about what's *really* going on. The more honest you can be with yourself and with someone you trust, the less shame will have a grip on you. Sometimes we want to paint a picture to others that things aren't so bad. Sometimes we have trouble seeing and admitting to *ourselves* how bad things really are. However, not facing up to the truth is a form of codependency. Codependency protects the addict and enables the cycle to continue, whereas honesty and accountability breaks the cycle.

Speaking of codependence, what about when *love* itself becomes an addiction? An obsession even? In addition to codependency, which is an unhealthy attachment to someone with an addiction, there is a condition called Love addiction or "obsessive love disorder,"[10] which is another attachment-related disorder. Similar to someone who has a relationship obsession, or attachment anxiety, the *obsessions* revolve around the person's love interest and the *compulsions* involve repetitive behaviors that are an attempt to relieve the obsessions.

Social media is one example of how being preoccupied with a love interest can fuel compulsions. For example, while obsessing about someone you love, or a former love interest, you may check their page compulsively, looking for updates on their status, such as what they are doing, who they are with, and what new pics or comments they're posting. You may find yourself wondering, *Are they with someone new? What is she like? Is she prettier than me?* I have fallen prey to this. In weak moments, I've even created a fake social media account to feed my obsession by checking on someone I was still emotionally attached to, even after the relationship ended. I definitely understand the grip of obsession!

Obsessional love is an emotional addiction that requires a similar detox process as a chemical addiction. If you have an addictive personality and are prone to obsessive thinking, your brain can latch onto people too quickly and become obsessive about them. The beginning stages of love are already quite addictive. Your brain is firing chemicals in a fast and furious way that really bonds you to someone. Having sex with them and/or fantasizing about them only increases that bonding experience. When the relationship ends, you can become even more obsessed with them. This is another form of addictive love, and access to social media only fuels it.

Prior to social media, when a relationship was over it was *over.* There wasn't a way to constantly see what that person was doing, to see their pics and updates, and know who they were with and where. You were forced to move on without glimpses into their day at the touch of a finger. Unless you heard through the grapevine what they were up to, or physically stalked them, you got no updates on their life. These days, you may be able to stalk someone in an instant on social media, but you don't get a true picture of their life. With the ability to photoshop, tweak, and filter every aspect of one's self, it's easy to say, "Hey look at me, life is grand without you." Every social media platform is literally at your fingertips, dangling the temptation to stalk and obsess over any number of people at any given time.

Obsessive love has been a theme in movies for years. In the movie *Fatal Attraction*, Glenn Close becomes obsessed with Michael Douglas to the degree that it takes over her life and ability to function. In this extreme case, she goes to insane lengths to break up his family and be with him. In a recent Netflix series about obsessive love, the main character "You" is obsessed about his love interest, incessantly stalking her and checking up on her at every turn. In the movie *Newness*, two people who found each other on a dating app become quickly infatuated and obsessed with each other, moving in together after barely knowing each other, and spending every waking moment together. As the movie progresses, they become bored with monogamy and, in turn, become obsessed with finding sexually-themed activities to spice things up, starting with flirting with other people in front of each other, having an open relationship, and ultimately cheating on each other, where things quickly take a nosedive.

Even if you don't have an addictive brain, you can still fall into the trap of obsession because humans were created to worship *something.* Whether it's a person, a substance, a music group, a child, a job—anything can become an object of worship. Yet often this is because we don't hear the Lord's gentle call to worship Him alone, which is the only way to find life and peace. Worshipping and obsessing over others *always* leads to a path of pain, because we weren't created to love anything (or anyone) more than God—and only *His* purpose for our lives will truly satisfy.

In the book *Obsessive Love*, Liz Hodgkinson talks about the addictive love she experienced with a man for over two decades of her life. It was a journey of suffering as she fought against the extreme mental angst in her soul, and sought healing as she tried to detach from the object of her obsession after approximately twenty years.

In the movie *Black Swan,* obsession is a theme throughout the film, not just the obsession with a person, but other unhealthy fixations too. The lead character, Nina, struggles with the obsession to be perfect in her career as a dancer. Thomas, her manager, struggles with the obsession to make Nina perfect. Lily, another dancer, wants to be like Nina and obsesses about taking her lead role.

We can be obsessed with beauty, perfection, a person, comparison, and the need to be desired. When obsession controls your mind, it leads to a rabbit hole of envy, pride, and fear. There are so many opportunities to obsess in this world, and all of them have the potential to drive us to some dark and lonely places in our hearts. They can also heap feelings of shame upon our souls. I've experienced the shame of obsessive love, both as the recipient and as the initiator. Because I have struggled with addiction, I am prone to latch on to things that give any sort of "high" including a person of interest, if I'm not careful.

I met Tyler on a crisp fall morning. He appeared in my life as fast and furious as a bolt of lightning. Just like a storm lights up the sky, he dazzled me with his charm, and before I knew it I was in the eye of the tornado, swept away by his compliments and professions of undying love for me. In hindsight, there were warning signs: the speed at which we were connecting, the inordinate amount of praise and promises. However, I didn't take cover. Instead, my heart latched on and quickly became obsessed with him in an unhealthy way.

Have you ever tried to paint red flags green? You really want to believe this person is who they say they are, yet deep down, your gut tells you otherwise. Ignoring your intuition is the same thing as painting red flags green. The problem is, sooner or later the paint fades and, once again, you're stuck with reality the red flag warned about.

One huge red flag I discovered along the way was that Tyler was a narcissist. The way I came to realize this was by talking to a friend who pointed it out to me. I told her about one of our recent interactions where he used gaslighting to make me doubt my perception of things and then blamed me for questioning him. It definitely felt abusive, but narcissism wasn't on my radar until my friend said, "Kristin, I think you're dating a narcissist."

As I began to research and learn more about this personality type, the writing was on the wall, and it was in bright red! Dating a narcissist involves a repetitive cycle of highs and lows, and it follows a very predictable pattern of *love-bombing, devaluing, discarding, hoovering*, repeat.

Love-bombing. In this process, the narcissist first draws you in with professions of their undying love for you, inordinate amounts of attention, and feelings of being their soul mate. If you really stopped to think about it (which you usually don't at this stage), you'd realize it's illogical for someone to feel they "know" and "love" you so completely after such a short period of time. Yet deep down, it's a narrative our hearts long to hear, so we often just soak it in without questioning or investigating further.

Then, before you know it, you're being *devalued.* This is when the confusion and *gaslighting* starts. The narcissist pulls out manipulative tactics to stay in control and keep you right where they want you, while always maintaining the upper hand. You will start to feel off-center, yet find reasons to rationalize the person's bad behavior because you long for the love-bombing stage to return. You'll try to please them, to make them happy, but it doesn't work.

Next, comes the *discard.* This is where they go into a tantrum and have fits of rage when they don't get their way. It doesn't even have to be over something big. It could be a very minor issue, but the next thing you know they're on a rant telling you all the things that are wrong with you before they cut you off, swearing to never talk to you again. Or maybe they ghost you. Just disappear out of the blue, without explanation or warning. You think they're gone for good this time.

Nevertheless, they always return. This is called *hoovering.* They come back around and suck you into their web like a vacuum cleaner, ready to play another round of relationship Twister, their favorite game. Narcissists love empaths. They are drawn to kind, caring people they can easily take advantage of. That's what Tyler did. He took advantage of my kindness and used it for his gain. Fortunately, I was able to detach and see the relationship for what it was— an illusion. A mirage in the desert that I kept chasing after, but as soon as I got close it disappeared. I had to fully detach in order to heal. Detaching was the hardest part of all— even harder than accepting reality. For those who struggle with obsessive love and relationship anxiety, detaching is the very last thing you want to do. Yet that's what it takes to become emotionally sober and free from heartbreak shame.

We need to learn the warning signs of toxic attractions by identifying them early on. Many people spend years of their life in this kind of dynamic, with lots of heartbreak shame to follow. You can form what's called a *trauma bond* with someone who is toxic. A trauma bond is an emotional bond that is formed with someone through a recurring cyclical pattern of *abuse, devaluing,* and *positive reinforcement.* It can be challenging to make sense of this pattern, especially when abusive actions alternate with kindness, yet that is exactly how the bond is formed. It creates feelings of shame when you feel like you can't stop the cycle. Fortunately, even if years of your life have been consumed by an abusive person, such as a narcissist, there is always hope. Once you learn their tactics, and how to heal from them, you can become empowered to withstand their abusive ways. Yes, the cycle can be intoxicating and addictive, but it *can* be broken. That's when healing for your heartbreak shame starts.

In the book *Attached*, Levine and Heller talk about how difficult breakups can be. They discuss a study that was done on the brain in which the same areas of the brain light up during a breakup as when you have a broken limb. That's how hard it can be to detach from someone you love, it feels just like a severed arm or leg. In addition, the degree of detachment difficulty correlates with your attachment style.

Attachment theory was first developed by Mary Ainsworth and John Bowlby in the 1950s. Your attachment style is a reflection of the relationship dynamics you had with your primary caregivers as a child. In adulthood, your attachment style depicts how you emotionally respond and behave toward others. There are four different styles; Anxious/Preoccupied, Avoidant, Fearful/Avoidant, and Secure. A person with an anxious attachment style is generally preoccupied in relationships with others. Someone with this style has a fear of separation or abandonment. The person with an avoidant attachment style can be withdrawn or guarded in relationships, and has a fear of being rejected. Someone with the combination type—fearful avoidant—exhibits a push-pull dynamic with others. Sometimes they want to be close and other times they want to pull away. They have difficulty with trust in relationships. When you have a secure attachment, you relate to others in a healthy way. There's a good balance between independence and closeness. There is no fear of intimacy, only a supportive, nurturing bond with one another.[11]

Learning about your attachment style, and how to detach from someone in a healthy way, can bring much healing and prepare you for a secure bond with a healthy individual.

Life Lesson

It is possible to be free from the grip of any addiction or obsession in your life. Not only is it possible, but that's what God wants for us. Because He wants it so much, He will give you strength every time you turn to Him. The more you seek God's presence in your weakness, the more He will protect you from the enemy's attacks!

Shame-Stopping Scripture: "If the Son sets you free, you will be free indeed (John 8:36, NIV). What do you want God to set you free from? Write how you envision Him setting you free.

____

____

____

____

____

HeartBRAKE #12

Freedom from Heartbreak Shame

At specific times in life, after you've been stuck and trapped in heartbreak shame for so long it's unbearable, you need to do whatever it takes to find the courage to fight for your dreams. There is nothing quite like the heartbreak of not completing your purpose when it's within your power to do. These are the moments you need to harness enough inner resolve to stop standing on the sidelines watching other people fulfill their goals and start fulfilling your own.

Consider this: Every product you consume is someone else's brainchild. When you watch TV, you're watching someone's creative concept. When look at social media, you're investing time in another person's billion-dollar venture. When you listen to music, you hear another's innovative idea at work. When you go to your job, you're working for someone who had a ground-breaking idea that they turned into a business. How much time do you spend looking at someone else's creative ideas instead of nurturing your own? God has placed an abundance of creativity within you—which you were born to share with the world.

Genesis 27–32 illustrates this concept as it depicts the lives of Jacob and Laban. Jacob worked for his uncle Laban for over twenty years (Genesis 31:41). During that time, Jacob experienced many delays on the way to fulfilling his dreams. One of those delays was a long wait for the woman he wanted to marry. Jacob loved Laban's daughter Rachel so he worked for seven years to earn her hand in marriage. Laban promised Jacob he could marry Rachel at the end of his commitment. However, after Jacob worked seven years, Laban deceived him by giving Jacob his daughter Leah to marry instead. Yet deception didn't stop Jacob from pursuing his heart's desire. He continued to fight for his dream to marry Rachel and worked seven more years so he could be with her (Genesis 29:20).

Jacob was a loyal, hard-working employee, just like you might be. Yet Jacob knew, after years of hard labor, that it was time to accelerate towards his calling and cultivate the creativity inside of him. He wanted to activate his creative ideas in a way that would sustain him financially, while using his God-given talents, instead of continuing to rely on Laban's resources and build Laban's fortune. Jacob was an entrepreneur at heart, but he was so busy working for Laban that he never gave his own dreams an opportunity to flourish.

As Jacob put the pedal to the medal, he gained enough acceleration to take a risk. He decided to use his creativity to produce a legacy that would bless others. While working on his uncle's land, Jacob learned how to manage livestock. He started with what he already knew how to do. He asked his uncle to allow him to choose from the spotted and speckled animals among his flock. Laban agreed, and Jacob took them down to the water trough where he devised a way for the animals to breed and reproduce in abundance, as they saw their reflection in the water. Jacob's creative idea worked. His invention caused a massive increase of cattle and was a great blessing in the life of Jacob and his family. The herds grew and grew until Jacob had his own business organizing and maintaining flocks of sheep, goats, and cattle (Genesis 30:37-43). Through Jacob's creative risk, he found a way to support his family, as well as his family's family. This is part of the legacy Jacob left on the earth as he chose to walk in the freedom of his calling.

Jacob used one simple principle. I call it the **BE SMART** principle: ***Boldly, Envision, See, Make, Ask, Reproduce, Tell.***

Boldly—Act.

Start.

Envision—Your future.

Picture what you truly want to see happen.

See—What's inside of you.

What are the creative gifts you've been given to fulfill your God-given purpose?

Make —It happen.

Once you have an idea, don't sit on it for too long or you will never take a risk. Step out of your comfort zone. Make an exit strategy OUT of dependence on others and INTO your creative venture.

Ask —For what you need.

What do you need to keep going? How can you ask others to help you? Don't be afraid to speak up and speak out, or to ask for help with your idea or your business!

Reproduce —Your vision.

What does God want to reproduce through you? What dream, product, or service, does He want to multiply through your creative gifts and talents? Writing? Singing? Teaching? Painting?

HeartBRAKE #12

Tell —Others.

Tell them what you have to offer them and how you want to support them. What God has put inside of you is meant to bless people. It's not just for you: it's for your family, your community, and the world. It's your creative legacy, your way of helping others know Him. It's your part in the Great Commission (Matthew 28:16–20).

Think about your gifts and talents. Reflect on how you can BE SMART with them. How can you use them to fully express who God created you to be, while pointing future generations toward Him?

Try answering these questions for yourself…

*How can I **boldly** take action?*

____

____

____

*What do I **envision** myself doing?*

____

____

____

*What need do I **see** in the world?*

____

____

____

*How can I **make** something happen?*

____

____

____

What do I need to ***ask*** *for to get started?*

____

____

____

What has God put inside of me to ***reproduce****?*

____

____

____

How can I ***tell*** *others about it?*

____

____

____

What is the ***legacy*** *I want to leave?*

____

____

____

Merriam Webster's Dictionary defines a *legacy* as "a gift (financial or material) left to another person, or group of people, after one dies."[12] Jacob passed down the flocks of animals, as well as the money they produced, to his family. That was the financial and material part of his legacy. The other part of his legacy was the creative gifts and talents he had within him. Jacob had the gift of business acumen and entrepreneurship. God changed Jacob's name to Israel, declaring him to be a prince and a leader who had influence with God and man (Genesis 32:28).

Let's continue to follow Jacob's legacy so we can see one of the ways it was reproduced through his children. Who was Jacob's legacy left to? It was left to his sons. Jacob had twelve sons who became the twelve tribes of Israel. Jacob's youngest son was Joseph. Joseph was sold into slavery by his brothers and sent to work in the house of Potiphar, one of Pharaoh's officials and the captain of the palace guard in Egypt. Joseph began his journey as a servant and a slave. However, when Joseph was thrown in prison after he was falsely accused of assaulting Potiphar's wife, he began having visions and dreams. Unbeknown to Joseph, God was preparing him to carry out the legacy of his father, Jacob, and fulfill his entrepreneurial calling.

Joseph was divinely inspired to store up grain for the years of famine that were about to ensue upon the earth. God gave Joseph a vision, an idea, and a strategy to carry it out, just like He wants to do with you and me. God showed Joseph exactly what He needed to do for his own and others' survival. That's what a business idea is. It is a God-given vision to help sustain yourself and your family, as well as bless those around you. Joseph was able to identify a problem (the famine) and find a solution to the problem (storing up grain to feed people during the famine). He left a material and spiritual legacy by being a godly leader, as well as a wise businessman in the community (Genesis 37, 39–47:26).

Creative writing endeavors are another example of how to leave a legacy. When my writing process for this book first began, I had a memory of writing as a small child. I distinctly remember penning the pages of my first manuscript with a friend. The book was about a little girl who went into a department store to shop. While she was in the store, she dropped a dollar bill, which fell inside the middle of a clothing rack. As she crawled around on the floor to find it, she entered a fantasy world filled with excitement and adventure. (I think I was heavily influenced by C.S Lewis!) The book I wrote as a child was a creative idea with the potential to be a blessing to other children. That's an example of an artistic gift flowing through me at an early age. That book was never published; however, the memory of it inspired me to start writing again as an adult. God has given me a second chance at a dream I never fulfilled when I was younger. What gifts has God put inside you, since you were a child, that He wants to reignite now?

Have your God-given gifts gotten run over on the road of life? Perhaps you started out with passion and ended up stuck in a place of pain. After experiencing repeated heartbreak shame, we forget about the book we started to write, the painting that's in the back of our closet, the dance we choreographed with our friends, the play we tried out for, the song we wrote, the idea we told a friend about over coffee, or the time we said, "Maybe I'll start my own business one day…" Before we realize it, that idea has faded into a distant memory.

Yet God has a way of reviving forgotten ideas and lost dreams.

One of the ways God brings buried hopes back to mind is through adversity. *Why does He do it this way*? you might wonder. Oftentimes, instead of reviving your dreams when you're at your best, when you have the most time, energy, or faith, He stirs up your creativity in the low places of life. I started this book during one of my most challenging heartbreaks. When it seemed like I was completely out of fuel, writing was my survival tool. I began pouring my pain onto pages, which turned into the words of this book. God has a wonderful way of revealing His glory and birthing our dreams through suffering.

What might God be asking you to create while you are on "E?"

God can revive the gifts inside you that were lost during the hard years and challenging places of your life. After all the crushing heartbreak shame you've endured, the dead battery of your dreams can be recharged. The time that was lost can be restored. Remember the scripture in Joel? "I will restore to you the years that the swarming locust has eaten, the crawling locust, the consuming locust, and the chewing locust, my great army which I sent among you" (Joel 2:25). There is nothing quite like going through a spiritual death followed by a creative renewal to bring forth new life. That's what happened to Jacob. All the years he spent suffering and serving suddenly catapulted him into a new beginning when he took the creativity God placed in his heart and manifested it through a herd of cattle.

Perhaps that's how God wants to jumpstart your dream, via your creative gifts and talents born through adversity. Activating your talents, by putting the pedal to the metal, will move you from point A to B. God can restore the joy that has been lost as you write your book, pen your song, launch your business idea, or start whatever venture He has put in your heart. This creative energy can move you from a place of heartbreak shame to a place of healing. So use your creative gifts and watch Him move you from park into drive. Through just one simple step of faith, God can change *not only* your life but *also* the lives of others through your creative ideas!

I remember a time I used the BE SMART principle. It was a time I sensed God was leading me out of my comfort zone, so I could use the gifts and talents that were dormant inside me. Honestly, it seemed like the most inopportune occasion. I was going through a difficult job transition and felt derailed by the unexpected detour taking place in my life. Yet I was asked to speak on the topic of human trafficking prevention at a woman's conference. I felt way under qualified. There were so many more knowledgeable presenters in this area, yet I was the one who'd been asked to do it. I love to speak and encourage others, but I often struggle with feelings of inadequacy when I'm engaging in public speaking. However, I knew in my gut that God wanted me to take on the assignment. As I stepped out in faith during a season of heartbreak, God used the gift of communication inside me to shed light on the dark world of human trafficking and persuade others to take part in its prevention. It was the BE SMART principle that I described earlier in action. Let's look at its practical application.

I *boldly* stepped out in faith to take on the assignment.

I *envisioned* myself speaking in front of others.

What need did I *see?* I saw a need for human trafficking awareness and prevention.

What did I *make* happen? I wrote my presentation, despite my insecurities, and committed to speaking at the conference.

What did I *ask* for? I asked for prayer support and practical assistance from a friend who attended the event with me.

What did I *reproduce*? I reproduced an important message: preventing human trafficking on a global scale. I did this by using my gifts of communication and speaking.

What did I *tell* others? I told them about the importance of being aware of the signs and how to get involved in the effort. I talked about God's heart for justice, which is an important component of the legacy I want to leave on earth: *Anyone can access and express their God-given dreams as they adventure into the unknown with Christ, despite the heartbreak shame they've endured.*

Jacob and Joseph's story is just one of many examples of leaving a legacy found in Scripture. Another account is seen through the friendship of Naomi and Ruth. As you read about what happened in their lives, listen to the ways God might be speaking to your heart regarding what kind of legacy He wants you to leave.

In the Book of Ruth, Naomi, Ruth's mother-in-law, is a grieving widow. The loss of her husband and two sons devastated her. She felt like God stripped everything away and left her alone in her despair. Naomi said, "For it grieves me very much for your sakes that the hand of the Lord has gone out against me!" (Ruth 1:13). Have you ever felt this way—like God's hand is against you, instead of *for* you? Fortunately for Naomi, the compassionate and committed love of her daughter-in-law, Ruth gave her the strength to keep going, despite her heartbreak shame. This story—and our own experience—shows us that God often sends the right person at just the right time to help us make it through the painful times in our lives. Who is—or has been—that person for you?

Like Jacob, Ruth needed a vision for provision. She needed a way to provide for herself and her mother-in-law, since they were both single women. Like Jacob, Ruth's vision was born from a place of despair. During Ruth's own grief and heartache, God gave her a divine impression that would bring forth change in her life and in the lives of others. Ruth had an idea to glean barley in the fields of the reapers, so she could get enough food to provide for herself and Naomi (Ruth 2:2). Ruth courageously acted on this idea, having no clue what God had in store for her. Not only would God provide for Ruth in abundance, He would also give her a Heavenly legacy to leave others.

Ruth was a hard worker, like Jacob. She worked from morning until night to see her vision come to pass (Ruth 2:7). Her concern was not just for herself, but for her family too. Imagine how Naomi must have felt as an older widowed woman, left to fend for herself. Ruth followed the vision for provision she had in her heart and saw it through to fruition. As the story continues, we see that Ruth happened to be working in the field of Boaz, who was related to Naomi's deceased husband and a mighty man of wealth (Ruth 2:1). While Ruth was gleaning in his field, Boaz had compassion on her and spoke a blessing over her (Ruth 2:12). He also offered Ruth extra barley from his field. "And when she rose up to glean, Boaz commanded his young men, saying, 'Let her glean even among the sheaves, and do not reproach her. Also let *grain* from the bundles fall purposely for her; leave *it* that she may glean' " (Ruth 2:15–16).

The steps of faith that Ruth took began with her seeing a need, which ignited the gifts she had within her. She then took courageous risks, which ultimately led to favor and provision from God. Ruth did what she could do in her natural strength. Then God intervened on her behalf. He had a sovereign, predestined plan to connect Ruth and Naomi, and to align them with Boaz, who would share his inheritance with them.

Ruth's story is similar to what God did for Jacob. He gave Jacob a vision, and then He provided for Jacob and his family as the creative idea flourished. What vision is God giving you? How do you think God wants to provide for you through that vision? As I've mentioned, a vision is often born through heartbreak and intended to produce a legacy that will be a blessing to others. What legacy do you want to leave?

When you seek Jesus, your Divine Navigator, He will guide you through life's detours and inspire you to activate your creative ideas, instead of allowing them to stay buried inside you. As your intimacy with Christ increases, so will your desire to serve others with your gifts and talents.

Who is God calling you to inspire? You might be enduring a heartbreak right now and struggling to believe you can make a difference in the world. You absolutely *can*! It's *through* your heartbreaks and pain that your legacy will be birthed. As you persist through every detour, delay, and dead end, God will accelerate your dormant dreams. Jesus *Himself* was a part of Ruth's legacy because she and Boaz eventually had a son who was part of the Lord's earthly lineage. Just imagine who or what God might produce through you!

If there is one question I run into time and time again as a counselor, it is, "How can I fulfill my purpose in spite of _________ setback?" (Fill in the blank with your own heartbreak.) *People want to know how to keep running the race of life when their hearts have been torn in two.* Sometimes heartbreaking, shame-fueling situations happen in our lives that are out of our control. Other times we make decisions that lead to heartbreaking outcomes. Whatever your situation may be, I want to encourage you NOT to let heartbreak stall your journey. Keep trusting God's sovereign plan for your life, and steer courageously toward your destiny. Don't let *any* kind of shame stop you!

In my office, I often see people who have stopped living their lives. The continual setbacks, broken dreams, and heartbreak shame have robbed them of their zeal for life. They wrestle with suicidal thoughts, thinking maybe it would be better for everyone if they weren't here anymore. They desperately want to end, medicate, or numb their emotional suffering and pain. They've stopped hoping for change and dreaming their dreams. Discouraging circumstances and cycles have gotten the best of them.

I've heard statements like, "Maybe this is just my lot in life. Nothing is ever going to change." Then they gradually stop believing things will ever be different. They become convinced that something is wrong with them, and that they will never break free from unhealthy situations or patterns.

Perhaps they've never been married, or they have been divorced one or more times. They conclude they don't know how to have lasting relationships with others. In defeat, they succumb to a life of loneliness and fear. They lose hope for having healthy, secure, attachments. I've also seen married men and women stop fighting for their marriages, thinking they must settle for unhappily ever after. I've watched people surrender to addictions such as pornography and drugs to numb their loneliness and pain. I too have chosen drugs over destiny, pain over purpose, hopelessness over healing. In their suffering, many people lose sight of God's vision and purpose for their lives, and as a result, *they simply stop living.*

I have looked in people's eyes and seen deep pools of emptiness and lifelessness. They are a shell of who they used to be. They are alive physically but spiritually dead. They've let heartbreak, fear, and shame take over. Maybe you can relate. Perhaps you have given up on your dreams ever coming to pass because of all the detours and delays you've experienced. Are you methodically going through each day, trudging through a nine-to-five job and numbing out with Netflix at night? Mindlessly repeating cycles can trap you into unhealthy ways of thinking, interacting, and living. These patterns can become so habitual that they even start to feel *normal* after a while. When numbness seems normal, you know you are flickering on fumes.

So how do you keep moving forward when life feels utterly hopeless? One way to gain forward momentum, which I mentioned in Chapter 5, is by inviting God to be the navigator of your life so He can empower you to leave a legacy. If you want to drive and thrive in your life, Jesus will help you stay the course until you fulfill your purpose. I have to admit, asking Jesus to be the navigator of my heart has been both the best and scariest decision I've ever made. It definitely took courage to entrust my life to Him. Yet knowing Christ has given me incredible endurance to get through life's twists and turns. I'm not talking about just going to church on Sundays. I'm talking about coming face-to-face with the fact that I am a sinner who needs a Savior. When I understood, believed, and aligned my life with this truth, I began the most incredible journey of a lifetime.

Jesus wants to be the navigator of *your* heart too. *Have you asked Him to be?* When you truly surrender to His leading, you will have peace knowing He is guiding you according to His radical and amazing plans for you on this earth, as well as in eternity, where you can be with Him forever.

Maybe you *have* asked God to navigate your heart, but you're still feeling discouraged by life's unexpected, heartbreaking setbacks and shame. It can be difficult to understand why God allows us to endure certain circumstances when we are wholeheartedly living our lives for Him the best we know how. There's no perfect answer for that question this side of Heaven, nor is there a perfect formula for surviving heartbreak.

However, sometimes having a realignment can help. In other words, realigning your heart with His through spiritual disciplines such as prayer, meditation, fasting, worship, reading God's Word, and surrounding yourself with people to encourage you. As you do this, it will reposition your heart to trust in His sovereign plans for you again. If you are in a place of discouragement, ask God *how* He wants you to realign your heart with His.

Another way to recharge your heart is through consistent self-care practices. Just like you need to take your car to the mechanic for a tune-up and oil change regularly, it's important to check in with your heart on a regular basis and listen to what it needs in order to stay healthy and whole. To give you an idea, a few self-care practices I engage in regularly include: counseling, life coaching, running, and reading, as well as spending quality time with friends. Journaling and meditation are also great ways to get in touch with your heart and slow yourself down, which is truly a challenge in our busy culture. As you practice self-care and stay connected with your Divine Navigator, your dreams and goals will become clearer. Taking care of yourself *first* keeps you healthier for others in the long run.

It's easy to lose hope when life throws you off course. Unfortunately, when you lose hope, you're more vulnerable to *losing touch* with your heart's desires completely. On top of that, if you're a people pleaser, losing faith in your own dreams will land you right in the middle of someone else's dream. If you have a hard time setting boundaries with people and saying no, you may end up living your life for someone else instead of yourself. It's important to stay connected to the God who dwells within your heart, so you don't lose touch with Him *or* yourself as you fight to fulfill your dreams.

As you make intentional time to heal from heartbreak shame, set goals for your future, and cast a fresh vision for your life, you are taking care of yourself and nurturing your God-given desires. Being good to yourself regularly will keep you on track. It will preserve your heart from burning out when you find yourself staring eye-to-eye with yet another unanticipated setback.

In addition, at certain times in life you must allow God to detach you from everything familiar, to move you out of a comfort zone and closer to your purpose. That's when you learn to walk by faith and not by sight (2 Corinthians 5:7). Walking by faith will keep you spiritually alive when walking by sight has killed you.

If things are changing in your life, like losing a job, a relationship, a place to live, or it seems like *everything* is being pulled out from under your feet, God could be orchestrating a faith-walk for you. If so, that means you are going to be on a very different path than the one you anticipated, and probably different from the people around you. You are going to think differently, act differently, and talk differently. It means you will be prompted by your Divine Navigator to do things that don't make sense to others, or sometimes even to yourself. I must admit, the scariest, yet most exhilarating times in my life have been the times I chose to walk by faith, not knowing where it would take me.

It was the time I quit my job and started my own business…

And God provided for me.

It was the time I stopped wrestling with God over what I wanted and said, "Okay Lord, You can have this."

And God's presence was with me in a way that can't compare with what I lost.

It was the time I obeyed His voice when it didn't make sense to do so. When everyone else said it was a foolish idea, but I did it anyway…

And God proved Himself (His voice) to be trustworthy.

It was the time I drove an old, beat-up car halfway across the country to where God was prompting me to go, praying I would reach my destination…

And by His grace, I made it.

It was the time I pursued my creative dream with hardly any money in my account…

And God supplied all my needs.

It was the time I moved overseas to follow my calling, wondering how I would survive in a foreign culture…

And I developed deep intimacy with Him that surpassed any earthly union I've ever had.

It's right now in my forties as, once again, I offer up another relationship heartbreak to God, after it didn't lead to marriage the way I'd hoped…

And, once again, Jesus promises to never leave me or forsake me (Hebrews 13:5)—and He doesn't.

During those times I've become fully alive again—the times when I've been shaken to the core of my being as I said "yes" to the God-sized adventure my heart needed to take to thrive and not die. It was then that my spirit soared to higher heights and deeper depths in Christ. It was those times that I *really* started living. It was during those faith-filled, fear-filled times, that I realized staying stuck had been draining me of the energy I needed to fulfill my God-given destiny.

One of those times in my life, I was traveling with my beloved mentor, Dr. Patricia Bailey, and she introduced me to a man named Dr. Myles Munroe. Dr. Munroe, just like Dr. Bailey, is dedicated to helping people navigate through detours to fulfill God's purpose for their lives. Dr. Munroe shared his own experience with heartbreaking detours. He shared how he often experienced racism growing up, which caused him to be derailed by other people's perspectives of him. He recounts the day he decided to stop believing the negative things other people said about him and write a different story for his life. With fresh hope, he took bold steps toward fulfilling his destiny, which included becoming the leader of a world-wide organization and the humble friend of many. He has authored numerous books that have been an inspiration to others.

Shortly after our introduction, I was saddened to hear of Dr. Munroe's death. It caught many people off guard because of the tragic and sudden way in which it happened. The redeeming part of the story, however, is that he was fulfilling his purpose at the time of his death. Not because he was well-known, but because he was leaving a legacy despite his heartbreaking experiences.

Are you willing to change the rest of your story? Or have you let heartbreak shame stop you?

You too can write a brand-new chapter in the story of your life. What do you want the next part of your life to say? Do you want it to be a repeat of the last five chapters, or a new chapter on how you started a fresh, faith-filled adventure with God?

What dreams are inside you? Do you want to start a business? Write a book? Have a family? It's not too late! Your path of adversity is birthing something new in you. *Your detours can lead you right to the doorstep of your destiny if you allow them to.* The Bible says, "Count it all joy when you fall into various trials, knowing that the testing of your faith produces patience. But let patience have *its* perfect work, that you may be perfect and complete, lacking nothing" (James 1:2). *What trial are you persisting through right now? What legacy is God whispering in your heart to leave? What imprint does He want to make on other people's lives through you, for His name's sake?*

Jacob, Joseph, Naomi, and Ruth all found purpose through their pain, and it was ultimately a great blessing to others. Ironically, the way I endured many of my setbacks, detours, discouraging days, and tear-filled nights, was to find someone else who was hurting worse than I was and walk alongside them. Whether I was listening to their story of untimely loss and grief or lending a hand through any number of devastating situations, I made myself available. I'm not sharing my experience to say, "look at what I have done for others." I'm sharing it with you as an example of how I was able to heal from my own heartbreak shame. Helping *is* healing. The times I stepped outside of my own suffering and into the shoes of someone else's have been very purposeful, meaningful, and fulfilling. It's what Jesus did. *Who do you think He wants you to come alongside of and help?*

As I close this chapter, I invite you to reflect upon how God is calling you to live, despite the heartbreak shame you've experienced. *What kind of legacy does He want you to leave?* Remember, no matter what kind of detours, delays, or dead ends you've experienced—or are currently experiencing—there is always hope for change. There is the hope that is found only in God's Word, His presence, and His promises to you. There is the hope of God's power to heal *all* your heartbreak shame. There is the hope that is discovered when we tap into our true gifts and calling and dare to leave a legacy, no matter how big or small.

As I was putting the final touches on this book, I experienced yet another heartbreak, one that reminded me of all the dashed hopes and delayed dreams I've experienced along the way. The many failed relationships, the loss of my childbearing years, the grip of addiction, toxic cycles, trauma, and seasons of shame. I sat in silence trying to accept the fact that my desires had to be crucified once again. Sometimes it feels like God is stripping every desire away. Whether they have been stripped away or surrendered along the way, I have learned (and continue to learn) how to break free from the shame *instead* of living in it. As I've walked through each heartbreak and embraced the healing process, I've learned to adopt a mindset that has freed me from idolizing earthly attachments and allowed me to walk in passionate pursuit of God and His purpose for me.

That mindset is that *God is inviting each of us to see things through His eternal eyes.* He wants us to remember that even if every single one of *our* plans and desires aren't fulfilled on this side of Heaven, all of *His* plans and desires for us *will be* fulfilled, both here and in eternity. God promises to fulfill the good work He began in us (Philippians 1:6). Isaiah 60 shows us a glorious picture of Heaven, where there will be no more heartbreak, no more tears, no more detours, delays, or dead ends, and no more heartbreak shame. There will be no more suffering of any kind—only rejoicing and triumph (Isaiah 60:19–21). Why? Because we will have reached our final destination. *The glory of God!* There will be no more setbacks or shame in His glory. Instead, we will be with Jesus forever, joyfully resting in His eternal presence. I hope the reminder of God's promises, found in His Word, will help you courageously embrace life from His perspective. His promises provide lasting freedom from heartbreak shame. They gave me that freedom, and they will do the same for you!

Life Lesson

Every setback and heartbreak shame you have experienced thus far, can produce within you a divine determination. It can give you a holy resolve to leave a legacy of endurance that shouts, "In spite of every single detour, delay and dead end, I will not give up! I will press on toward my dreams until God's purpose in me is complete.

Shame-Stopping Scripture: "For I know the thoughts that I think toward you, says the Lord, thoughts of peace and not of evil, to give you a future and a hope" (Jeremiah 29:11). What is the legacy God wants you to leave for others? Write about it here.

____

____

____

____

____

I admonish you, *keep on living for Christ, my friend!* Live by enduring every heartbreak shame, disappointment, detour, delay, and dead end, trusting in God's sovereign plan for your life. Live by embracing hope, against all painful odds, remembering who God is and who He is calling you to be. Live by leaving a legacy that will shine brightly into eternity. Live by saying goodbye to shame, breaking free from the pain, and embracing the joy of becoming ALL you're meant to be in Christ.

I believe in you!

ABOUT THE AUTHOR

Author Kristin Frank's passion for writing began as a child, as she grew up in Newark, Delaware. She was raised Catholic, and despite a bit of a rebellious streak, she really wanted to understand and help people. That desire led her to earn a B.A. in Psychology from the University of Delaware.

Although she didn't think the work was quite right for her, one of her first jobs was a teaching assistant. In that environment, she was blessed with a good relationship with a teacher colleague and friend, Dawn, who began sharing her faith with Kristin. As Kristin's curiosity was piqued, and she began reading the Bible for herself. As she read, the verse, My sheep know my voice and they follow me, She asked God, "Am I one of your sheep?" At home, when she was 25, and laying in a bathtub, He revealed to her that she was indeed one of His sheep. He also revealed the importance of baptism. She finds it humorous that He taught her about baptism in a bathtub! Kristin was baptized by immersion shortly thereafter.

As she continued to hear God's voice, He led her step-by-step on a journey of faith through career transitions. Through it all, she longed to be married and have a family. As you've read in this book, those desires sometimes won out over what she was learning about God and how He was guiding her.

The more she surrendered and learned, the more she wanted to understand how to practically help herself and others heal emotionally and spiritually. To that end, she earned a Master's in Pastoral Counseling from Loyola University Maryland, along with her LCMHC credentials, in 2008. She also earned a life coaching certification (CLC) from the Institute of Life Coach Training. Along the way, she went overseas to do missionary work.

Kristin opened her own counseling and coaching practice in 2019 in Greensboro, North Carolina. When she wrote this book, she had been practicing counseling for 10 years.

Kristin has also spoken at conferences and taught seminars on creating a balanced vision for your life, fulfilling forgotten dreams, raising awareness of mental health in the church, healing past hurt and pain, and recognizing unhealthy relationships, along with other topics.

Her future plans involve branching out from one-on-one counseling to continue more writing, speaking, and traveling.

To connect with Kristin, please visit kristinfranks.com, or connect with her on one of her social media accounts below.

If you need counseling, visit www.psychologytoday.com. Therapists are available all around the U.S. Kristin is listed on this resource as well.

Facebook: Kristin Franks

Instagram: Kristin_cares

Pinterst: kristincares

LinkedIn: Kristin Franks

ACKNOWLEDGMENTS

Writing a book has proven to be the greatest joy and challenge of my spiritual journey thus far. Without the ongoing and continual support of my family and friends, it would not have even been possible. For all of you, I am eternally grateful! My greatest appreciation goes to Christ, who has been my constant, faithful, loving companion through it all. His Spirit and grace is the sole reason and inspiration for each and every part of my story. Other immense gratitude goes to;

Dr. Patricia Bailey: My dear mentor, friend, and spiritual mom, you have completely shaped and transformed my life through your love, wisdom, incredible faith, and heart for the widow, orphan, refugee, and the poor. By watching the way you live and love like Christ, I continue to be in awe and deeply moved to walk in your footsteps as you follow hard after God. I love you so much, and I'm forever grateful for you!

Kim Aldrich: Without your continual loving support, cheerleading, fantastic coaching, and amazing editing, this book would not have been written! You have a heart of gold and an endless supply of compassion and kindness. I cherish the days we wrote together and grew as authors. You are a rare and invaluable gem of a woman, and I appreciate you so much!

Sabrina Isenhour: You are an incredible person and beautiful friend. Thank you for your endless patience and encouragement while I was writing this book. You had an intimate look at my refining process and have stuck with me through it all. Your Godly wisdom and insight greatly impacted my writing. I am forever grateful for you and for our friendship!

My family: To my Dad (Jack) my mom (Mary), my brother (Steve) and my sister (Alicia), and also to my grandmother (Kitty Welikonich), I am so grateful to have all of you in my life. You have helped me become the person I am today! Thank you all so much for your love and support along the way.

Jerome Daley: If it wasn't for your book coaching group, this manuscript would not be published! It was a fantastic opportunity to nurture my passion for writing. Your coaching support and writing expertise changed my life. Thank you so much, Jerome.

Faithful Friends: Thank you all for cheering me on and seeing me through this publishing process! Sabrina Johnson Coates, Ann McDonald, Jennifer McIntyre, Ben and Joy Shamberger, Keisha Barnes, MaryDale Worboys, Barbara Vaughn, Mary Roberts, Traci Collins, Chris Ausbon, Folasade Scott, Kalyne Reid, Lonya Wiggins, and Daniel Newby—I am so grateful for all of you!

Daniel and Patty Bausum: To my pastors Daniel and Patty, I felt loved and cherished by you right from the very start. Little did I know I would have a special connection with you because of your daughter Joy, who gave her life to share the Gospel. As soon as I found out there was a book written in her honor, my spirit leapt inside. You inspired me to keep writing through all of the obstacles I faced. Thank you for your persevering spirit, generous heart, and agape love!

Loral Pepoon: Loral, I cannot thank you enough for taking this project on at the time you did! Meeting you was truly a divine connection. I am honored to have you as my publisher. Your heartfelt encouragement and motivation helped see this through to completion. Thank you, Selah Press, for your excellent work and vision to help new authors.

Anna Floit: You helped turn the beginning stages of my manuscript into a real story that speaks to the heart of others. I love your editing style, and I appreciate all of your hard work and effort at the beginning of this process. Without your insight and guidance, this book would still be a diary!

Christine Dupre: We started creating a vision for the cover years ago, and then you promptly picked up right where we left off, without hesitation! Your abounding energy and enthusiasm for my work, coupled with your amazing talent at design, helped make my dream a reality. Thank you for sharing your gift with me, Christine!

And last, but definitely not least: to all those who prayed for me while I was deep in the writing trenches, I greatly appreciate your silent prayers and guidance along the way. You are the reason I was able to persevere when I felt like giving up. Your prayers paved the way for me to leave a legacy for others. Thank you all, so very much!

NOTES

1. *Merriam-Webster.com*, , https://www.merriam-webster.com/dictionary/pileup, s.v. "pileup" (n).

2. *Wikipedia: The Free Encyclopedia,* https://en.wikipedia.org/wiki/Love_bombing, s.v. "Lovebombing," accessed September 21, 2021.

3. Allison Abbott, "COVID's mental-health toll: how scientists are tracking a surge in depression," *Nature* 590 (February 3, 2021): 194–195, https://doi.org/10.1038/d41586-021-00175-z.

4. Harvill Hendrix, "What is Imago?" *Harville and Helen*, https://harvilleandhelen.com/initiatives/what-is-imago, accessed July 7, 2020.

5. "What is Sexual Violence?" The Center for Family Justice, https://centerforfamilyjustice.org/faq/sexual-violence/, accessed September 28, 2021.

6. James Strong, *The New Strong's Exhaustive Concordance of the Bible, Words in the Greek Testament* (Nashville: Thomas Nelson Publishers, 1995), 15, s.v. "deliverance" (n.).

7. Marilyn Hickey, *The Power of Prayer and Fasting: 21 Days That Can Change Your Life* (New York: FaithWords, 2006), various.

8. *Lexico*, powered by Oxford,, accessed Sept. 21, 2021 https://www.lexico.com/en/definition/temptation, s.v. "temptation" (n.).

9. Elizabeth Hartney, BSc, MSc, MA, PhD, "Is Sex Addiction Real, a Joke, or Just an Excuse?" *Very Well Mind,* updated March 14, 2021, https://www.verywellmind.com/is-sex-addiction-a-real-addiction-22452.

10. "What Is Obsessive Love Disorder?" *Healthline*, https://www.healthline.com/health/obsessive-love-disorder.

11. Kelly Gonsalves, "What Is Your Attachment Style? Attachment Theory, Explained," mindbodygreen.com, https://www.mindbodygreen.com/articles/attachment-theory-and-the-4-attachment-styles.

12. *Merriam-Webster.com*, https://www.merriam-webster.com/dictionary/legacy, s.v. "legacy" (n.).

Made in the USA
Columbia, SC
19 November 2021

49135539R00111